On the Road

Tourism English for Travelers

1

Joseph Henley

✷ CENGAGE

Australia • Brazil • Canada • Mexico • Singapore • United Kingdom • United States

On the Road 1
Tourism English for Travelers
Joseph Henley

Senior Director, ELT Asia :
Michael Cahill

Publisher, Asia ELT:
Edward Yoshioka

Assistant Manager, Publishing:
Melody Chiu

Editor:
Percy Chang

Senior Production Executive:
Evan Wu

Compositor:
Cynthia Chou

Cover Designer:
Evan Wu

ISBN: 978-4-86312-402-8

Cengage Learning K.K.
No. 2 Funato Building, 5F
1-11-11 Kudankita, Chiyoda-ku
Tokyo 102-0073, Japan

Cengage Learning is a leading provider of customized learning solutions with office locations around the globe, including Singapore, the United Kingdom, Australia, Mexico, Brazil, and Japan.

Locate your local office at **www.cengage.com**

To learn more about Cengage Learning Solutions, visit **www.cengageasia.com**

Printed in Singapore
Print Number: 01   Print Year: 2023

On the Road
Tourism English for Travelers

If you've ever been lost for words while traveling to another country, the *On the Road* series could be the books for you. There are two books, which are aimed at elementary and pre-intermediate level students. The overall aim of the series is to give English learners the basic tools they'll need to effectively communicate in English on their vacations.

Each *On the Road* book contains 15 teaching units, and they've been carefully designed to cover everything you need to know, from booking your trip to ordering room service to buying souvenirs. The units are grouped into five similarly themed sections. At the end of each section, there's a review unit with listening and reading questions to ensure smooth progress through the book.

The *On the Road* series deals with all four skills: reading, writing, speaking, and listening. There are two dialogues in each unit for you to listen to. They deal with real-life situations and introduce helpful new words and phrases that should make life easier for you when traveling overseas. There are reading comprehension passages with questions that target both major themes and specific pieces of information. A different grammar point is covered in each unit, and you'll have the chance to practice using them in the writing section. There are also lots of opportunities to speak, as each unit begins with a simple speaking exercise and finishes with two more in-depth activities.

While the central aim of these books is to help learners deal with overseas travel situations comfortably and confidently, the *On the Road* series provides a strong foundation in English for all students, no matter how often they want to take vacations.

For vacation English and a great, all-round learning experience, you should pick up this series of books and pack it up every time you're *On the Road*!

Table of Contents

Unit 1

My Travel Plans

By the end of this unit, you will be able to do the following:

✈ Compare travel plans
✈ Talk about activities you like to do
✈ Ask for travel advice
✈ Make a schedule

✈ Before We Go

Look at the following activities that people enjoy doing on vacation. Match each word from the box with the activity.

| hiking | sailing | sightseeing | skiing | swimming | visiting museums |

❶

❷

❸

❹

❺

❻

✈ Useful Expressions

- I'd like to take a vacation *in the city* because I like to *visit the museums*.
- The *beach* looks best to me because I like *surfing*.
- I enjoy *hiking*, so I think I would like a vacation *in the mountains* the best.

Conversation 1

Track 2 Anna is planning a trip to Europe, and her friend Ben is helping her compare travel plans. Listen to the conversation and fill in the missing words.

Anna: I'm trying to decide if I want to be a part of a tour or just travel on my own.

Ben: Well, what do you like best when you travel?

Anna: I ❶ _____ time in each place I visit, so I ❷ _____ my own schedule.

Ben: That sounds like you prefer to travel alone.

Anna: Well, traveling alone is more fun, but it is also more difficult.

Ben: Do you ❸ _____ everything yourself?

Anna: It is easier to let someone else do it, but then I may not like everything on the itinerary. I think I ❹ _____ the trip myself.

Ben: Is it safe to go alone?

Anna: Going on a group tour might be safer, but I'll be OK alone if I make smart choices about where I stay and about transportation.

Ben: Well, the first choice you have to make is about where you're going.

Anna: I know! That's the exciting part. I ❺ _____ at all of the guide books. I ❻ _____ my time and ❼ _____ a lot of research. I think I'll check out some European travel forums and see what people recommend.

Words to Remember

Use the words in the box to complete the sentences.

| schedule | itinerary | transportation | research | book | group tour | guide book | forum |

1. We need to make a trip _____ first so we can organize our _____ methods.

2. Leila wants to take a trip around the U.S. so she spends lots of time on the _____ .

3. Monica likes the _____ the travel agent planned so she's going to sign up for that _____ .

4. Should I bring _____ when I travel? This Internet travel _____ suggests I just take brochures the local tourism bureau provided to travel light.

5. I have _____ a flight to New York next month.

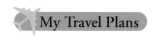

 My Travel Plans

Reading

 Track 3 Read Anna's entry and the responses to her questions on a European travel forum below.

Backpack Europe Forum

 Advice Needed!   03/07/2013 11:42 AM

Anna S newbie Loc: California
Hi! I'm planning a backpacking trip through Europe, and I need to know the best countries to see. I enjoy sightseeing in old cities. I also like spending time outside, and I love hiking. I only have one month to travel, so I need ideas. Thanks!

 Re: Advice Needed! [Re: Anna S]   03/07/2013 4:08 PM

Backpack Brian member Loc: New York
You should go to the United Kingdom, France, Italy, and Spain. I enjoy visiting museums, and these countries have some of the best. I dislike hiking and stuff, so I don't know where you should go for outdoor activities.

 Re: Advice Needed! [Re: Anna S]   03/08/2013 7:59 AMPM

TravelCutie newbie Loc: Amsterdam
Come to Holland! If you like riding bikes, it's a great place to visit. I guess the United Kingdom is also good, if you don't mind eating bad food. JK! :-P I enjoyed going to Spain last year, and France is great. You might want to check them out, too!

Re: Advice Needed! [Re: Anna S]   03/16/2013 10:34 PM

Sandman member Loc: France
I'm traveling through France and Spain right now, and I love it! There are so many beautiful beaches in the south. Everyone I know loves catching some sun and swimming here. If you enjoy swimming, sailing, and sightseeing, France is the best place to go! I hear Austria has some cool mountains for hiking, though.

Give It a Try

Read the forum again and choose the best response to each of the following questions.

1. Where is the forum?
   a. It's on the Internet.
   b. It's held in the U.S.
   c. Anna held it.
   d. It's somewhere in France.

2. What is NOT true about BackpackBrian?
   a. He's a backpacker.
   b. He's a member of the forum.
   c. He's a backpack seller.
   d. He lives in New York.

3. What activities does Anna like to do?
   a. She enjoys sightseeing.
   b. She likes outdoor activities.
   c. She loves hiking.
   d. All of the above.

Conversation 2

Track 4 After some help from her new online friends, Anna has decided on which countries to visit. Listen as she and her friend Scott make a schedule for what she will do in one of the countries, France. Listen to the conversation and fill in the missing words.

Scott: OK, so you're going to take the train from London to Paris ❶ _____, right?

Anna: That's right. It leaves London ❷ _____ and arrives in Paris ❸ _____.

Scott: That's still pretty early ❹ _____. In fact, you're getting to Paris ❺ _____. Will you go get something to eat right away?

Anna: Well, I should probably check in at my hostel.

Scott: Where are you staying?

Anna: Near the train station. It's in an old building that was built ❻ _____!

Scott: That's amazing! I bet it will be crowded ❼ _____.

Anna: Yeah, I think that's its busiest season. That's why I want to make sure that they don't give away my room to someone else!

Scott: So what will you do the next day?

Anna: Well, I arrive ❽ _____, and I have a bus tour of Paris booked ❾ _____. It ends at the Louvre. I can't wait to explore that museum!

Scott: And what will you do ❿ _____?

Anna: I don't know yet. I could go to an outdoor market, take a cruise on the Seine, or go to the top of the Eiffel Tower. With so much to see, I can't imagine that I will be bored!

Words to Remember

Use the words in the box to complete the sentences.

dinnertime	hostel	amazing	crowded	explore	market	cruise

1. Janet couldn't wait to _____ the city the moment she settled in this cheap _____.

2. Larry found some _____ gifts for his friends in the nearby _____.

3. The couple went out early and didn't come back until _____.

4. Jenny fancied a romance on this Mediterranean _____ and she actually found her Mr. Right!

5. There is a festival going on so the city is _____ with tourists.

Get It Right

Pretend that you are Anna, and you are writing a postcard to a friend about your time in Paris. Use *will* and *would* to describe your trip.

Dear Scott,

Hello from Paris! I'm having a great time here! I arrived on Thursday at 6:17 and have been very busy since then.

After checking into my hotel at 7:00 in the evening, I went to dinner. On Friday ...

_____

_____

_____

_____

Best wishes,

Anna

Scott Huser
810 Main Street
Grapevine, Texas 76051
U.S.A.

Grammar Bite

Will and *would* are auxiliary verbs, and are always followed by a main verb. *Will* is used to express desire, preference, choice, or consent. For example:

* I *will* do the job.
* *Will* you stop doing that?

Will can also be used to express that something will happen in the future. For example:

* It *will* be hot tomorrow.
* The song *will* reach number one on the charts.

It can also be used to express capacity, or capability. For example:

* The baseball stadium *will* seat 10,000 people.

Would is the past form of *will*. It can also be used to express a desire.

* I *would* like some more food, please.

It can be used to express possibility.

* I *would* be smiling if I were you.

Give It a Try

Fill in the blanks with either *will* or *would*.

1. It _____ rain tomorrow.

2. When I was young we woke up early. We _____ get up at 6 a.m.

3. I _____ like a glass of water, please.

4. I _____ be serious if I was in your position.

5. The theater _____ seat 500 people.

🎈 Prepare Yourself

Look at the cities and the attractions and activities of each city. Use the Internet to research any sites or places that you aren't familiar with.

- Anne Frank House
- Diamond Museum
- visit outdoor markets
- bicycle near canals
- take boat tour on canals

- Tower of London
- British Museum
- Buckingham Palace
- see play
- take cruise on River Thames

- Eiffel Tower
- Louvre Museum
- Arc de Triomphe
- go shopping
- eat at café in Latin Quarter

- Colosseum
- Sistine Chapel
- Pantheon
- eat gelato
- throw coin in Trevi Fountain

🎈 Activity

In the cities above, what would you like to see and to do? Circle the items that interest you. Then, use the space below to write one more city and three things that you would like to see and to do there.

- City: _Paris_
- Places to see: _Eiffel Tower_
- Things to do: _going shopping_
  I will arrive in Paris on July 24th. On the first day, I will visit the Eiffel Tower. Next, I will go shopping.

🎈 Useful Expressions

- I will arrive in *Rome* on *July 26th*. At *10:00* on the first day, I will *go to the Vatican Museum*.
- Next, I will go to *the Pantheon*. There, I can *have lunch*.
- I really want to visit the *Spanish Steps* because I love *watching people*.

13

Unit 2
What Should I Bring?

By the end of this unit, you will be able to do the following:

→ Describe the things you will bring with you on a trip
→ Ask questions about what you should bring with you and what you should leave behind
→ Provide some basic packing tips to others
→ Talk about packing for a trip with friends

Before We Go

Look at the pictures below. Each picture shows a different item you might need when packing for a vacation. Match the words from the box to the correct item.

| suitcase | backpack | clothing | toothbrush | sunglasses | passport |

❶

❷

❸

❹

❺

❻

Useful Expressions

- What is in your *suitcase*?
- I have a *hairdryer* in my *suitcase*.

- What is that next to the *toothbrush*?
- I think you should also bring your *sunglasses*.

Conversation 1

Track 5 Carl is packing for a trip to the U.K., and is trying to figure out what he should bring with him. His friend, Leanne, is helping him pack. Listen to the conversation and fill in the missing words.

Carl: I'm not sure what I should ❶ _____ me. I've never traveled before.

Leanne: I've gone backpacking lots of times. I can help you figure out what to ❷ _____ .

Carl: OK, so far I've got a change of clothes, my toothbrush, my sunglasses...

Leanne: Did you bring a book to read? I like to have a book for long train or bus rides.

Carl: Good idea. What else?

Leanne: You might want to bring a ❸ _____ , too. It's very ❹ _____ because you can use it instead of carrying your suitcase around everywhere.

Carl: I didn't think of that. Oh, I almost forgot. I'd better ❺ _____ a few pairs of shoes, too. I wouldn't want to be caught without the right pair of shoes.

Leanne: That's not really ❻ _____ . Just bring one or two different pairs. If you really need another one, you can pick it up on the road.

Carl: Good thinking. What about my toothbrush and all this other stuff I use in the bathroom? It's just scattered all over the place.

Leanne: Get a good shaving kit. It can prevent you from losing anything, and it's easy to ❼ _____ . My boyfriend always brings his along.

Carl: I'm just worried I'll leave something behind. There are so many things I want to bring.

Leanne: I always find it's best to ❽ _____ . Remember, if you forget something, you can easily replace it when you're overseas.

Words to Remember

Use the words in the box to complete the sentences.

day pack	bring with	useful	throw in	practical	pack	carry	travel light

1. Paul carries a small backpack because he likes to _____ .
2. It's not _____ to bring 30 shirts on a one-week vacation.
3. Jim wants a smaller suitcase, because his is too big to _____ .
4. Francine left her big backpack at the hostel, and just brought her _____ with her.
5. Ben always makes a list of things he needs before he _____ his backpack.

 Reading

Track 6 Read this blog on packing tips, written by a travel expert who has been around the world.

To Pack, or Not to Pack?

So, you're about to head out on your dream vacation. The only question is, what are you going to bring with you? But the real question is, what should you leave behind? Trust me, I've traveled around the world, and what is the one thing I see most often?

Tourists carrying around too much stuff. It can ruin an entire vacation. If you've got a heavy pack or suitcase to carry around everywhere, it's going to put you in a bad mood. This is especially true if you're traveling through an area with a suitcase and the roads or sidewalks are bad. You won't even be able to roll it along. So, after you've packed everything you think you need, take a second look in your suitcase or backpack. Go through each item and ask yourself two questions:

1. Can I live without it?
2. Can it be easily replaced on the road?

If you answer "Yes" to both questions, leave it behind. If you bring it along, it will just clutter up your life. Remember, traveling is about exploring, and you won't want to do much exploring if you've always got too much stuff with you. Carrying too much weight can lead to muscle pain, and even serious injury. Just pack a few essentials: a few changes of clothing, toiletries, and maybe a small netbook PC if you really need to do some work or send e-mails on the road. And of course bring

all your essential travel documents with you. Other than that, what do you need? Nothing. Anything else can be purchased on the road if need be. Fewer complications equals less stress, and that applies to packing. The main thing to remember is, less is more.

Give It a Try

Based on the blog, choose whether these sentences are True or False?

1. You should pack as many things as you can.   True / False
2. Ask yourself two questions before you pack.   True / False
3. If you answer "Yes" to both questions, bring the item with you.   True / False
4. The more complications, the more stress.   True / False
5. Carrying a lot of things is good for your muscles.   True / False

Conversation 2

Track 7 Carl has arrived in London and has checked into a shared room in a hostel. As he unpacks, he notices that he has left something very important behind. A fellow traveler, Danielle, lends a hand. Listen to the conversation and fill in the missing words.

Carl: Let's see here...I've got my favorite shirt, my passport, and... Oh no!

Danielle: What's wrong? Is there anything I can do?

Carl: I forgot my ATM card. Oh, this is so stupid. How could I ❶ _____ something so ❷ _____ ?

Danielle It's OK. It's actually not that big of a deal. Are you sure you forgot it? Maybe it's just ❸ _____ somewhere in your suitcase.

Carl: No, I don't think so. How am I going to get cash? I only have enough with me for the first few days.

Danielle: If your bank has a branch here, you can just go get a ❹ _____ card.

Carl: No, I don't think there's a branch here. I'll have to call home to arrange for a new card to be ❺ _____ here. That could take weeks!

Danielle: Hold on, let's take one more look around in there. I thought I saw something. Do you mind?

Carl: Not at all. Please, go ahead. I ❻ _____ everything else. How could I forget something like that?

Danielle: You sure did bring a lot of ❼ _____ . No wonder you can't find anything in here.

Carl: Yeah, my friend told me to pack light, but I guess I didn't follow her advice very well. Wait, is that my card?

Danielle: Yup, it was right here under your...is that a computer keyboard? Why on earth did you bring so many ❽ _____ ?

Words to Remember

Use the words in the box to complete the sentences.

misplace	forget	important	replacement	remember	stuff	send	thing

1. If you lose something when you travel, it's easy to buy a _____ .
2. Don't pack something if it's not _____ .
3. Mark bought some souvenirs during his trip, and he _____ them home through the mail.
4. Roger's backpack was full, so he had to get rid of some of his _____ .
5. Don't _____ your passport whenever you go overseas.

17

Get It Right

Pretend that you are Carl and you are writing to a friend from London. In the letter, you will give your friend some advice about what they should bring on their own trip abroad. Use at least three countable, and three uncountable nouns in the letter.

> Dear Peter,
>
> Greetings from London,
>
> Things are going very well here in London. I heard you are going to be taking your own trip overseas soon. I thought I'd offer you some advice about what to pack. Maybe you can avoid making some of the same mistakes I did. First of all, don't forget to bring...

_____

_____

_____

_____

Grammar Bite

There are two different kinds of nouns, countable, and uncountable. Countable nouns can have a singular or plural numeral before them, while uncountable nouns cannot. We often have to use countable and uncountable nouns when we describe what we are packing for a trip.

Countable: *house, pen, dog, ball, …*

Examples:

- How many *houses* are on this street?
- Frank ordered *a cup of coffee.*
- How many *pens* do you have?
- The *dogs* are very hungry.

Uncountable: *information, news, coffee, truth, furniture, …*

Examples:

- There is a lot of *information* here.
- Have you read the *news*?
- Would you like some *coffee*?
- I want to know the *truth*.

Give It a Try

Choose which form of the noun in each sentence is correct.

1. I put some *(shirt / shirts)* in my backpack.
2. Don't forget to bring a *(comb / combs)* on your trip.
3. I didn't remember to bring my *(toothbrush / toothbrushes)* with me.
4. Can you lend me some *(money / moneys)*? I can't find my ATM card in my suitcase.
5. I need to buy new *(luggage / luggages)*. Mine is falling apart.

Prepare Yourself

Look the pictures below. On the floor, you'll see a number of items laid out, waiting to be packed into a suitcase.

Activity

With a partner, take turns asking and answering the following questions about the pictures above.

1. Which of these items would you bring with you on a trip?

2. Which of these items would you leave behind?

3. If you could bring just three items of those in the picture, which would you choose and why?

4. Do you think this person is bringing too much stuff, or not enough? Explain your answer.

 Useful Expressions

- I could not live without *a hairdryer*.
- *A water bottle* would be useful on any trip.
- I would bring *socks* and *a toiletry bag*.
- I would also bring along *some books*.

Unit 3

Catching a Plane

By the end of this unit, you will be able to do the following:

→ Talk about going through an airport
→ Manage a conversation about boarding a plane
→ Get through customs and passport control
→ Ask for information about flight departures and arrivals

 **Before We Go**

Look at the pictures in an airport terminal below. There are several places marked with the numbers 1-6. Match these places to the correct words from the box.

check-in desk	moving sidewalk	security screening
customs and immigration	baggage claim	duty free

❶

❷

❸

❹

❺

❻

Conversation 1

Track 8 David is heading to the airport. He's never taken a flight before, and his friend Justine is letting him know what to expect.

David: So, my ❶ _____ leaves tomorrow. I'm actually a bit nervous. I've never even been to an ❷ _____ before.

Justine: Don't worry. There's nothing to it. These days, getting through the airport is really convenient.

David: What do I do first?

Justine: Well, first you'll get dropped off at the ❸ _____ ❹ _____. Go inside and find your airline's check-in desk. They'll give you your ticket, but don't forget your passport. You can't get your ticket without it.

David: OK, what's next? ❺ _____ screening, right?

Justine: That's right. You'll have to go through a metal detector so the security officers can make sure you don't have anything dangerous with you.

David: And after that?

Justine: Then you go through ❻ _____. That's where they stamp your passport and send you on your way.

David: That does sound pretty easy.

Justine: It's a breeze. Just be sure to have all your important travel documents with you, such as your flight ❼ _____. And your ❽ _____, if you have one.

David: I've already printed off my confirmation and have it in a safe place.

Justine: Great, then you're all set to go!

Words to Remember

Use the words in the box to complete the sentences.

flight	airport	departure	security
confirmation	e-ticket	terminal	passport control

1. Paul had to rush to the airport to catch his _____.
2. To get around the country by bus, Penny goes to the bus _____ for information.
3. John booked his flight online and printed off his _____.
4. Jim was stopped at the _____ check because he had some change in his pocket.
5. You should always call to make a _____ of your flight before departure.

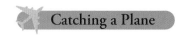
Reading

Track 9 Read this statement from airport officials on new security regulations and services.

Attention Valued Passengers,

We here at Thompson International Airport would like to thank you for continuing to fly with us over the years. You've helped us become the busiest airport in the state, and we couldn't have done it without you. With that in mind, we will be introducing some new security measures in the coming months. These measures will be undertaken with your safety and convenience in mind, so please bear with us. First of all, we will be putting some new equipment in place to provide added security. This equipment includes

state-of-the-art machines which can see through clothing. This is to ensure that no dangerous items are brought aboard flights leaving Thompson International. Should you not wish to pass through one of these machines, simply state your preference to one of our security personnel. They will arrange for you to be searched by a person instead.

Secondly, we will be installing machines that will allow you to check in without having to line up at one of our check-in counters. Taking advantage of this service requires that you register online, and provide us with some key information. We promise that your personal information will not be passed on to any third party. Lastly, for the time being it is still prohibited to bring any liquids above 200 ml aboard our flights. Thanks for your attention, and thank you for continuing to fly out of Thompson International.

Give It a Try

Based on the statement, circle True or False for the following sentences.

1. Liquids above 200 ml in size can now be brought aboard flights.   True / False
2. People can now check in without having to go to a check-in counter.   True / False
3. New equipment has been put into the airport.   True / False
4. These new measures are only for peoples' convenience.   True / False
5. People can refuse to pass through the machines which see through clothing.   True / False

 Conversation 2

Track 10 David is now at the airport, and is at the check-in counter speaking to Sally, an airline employee.

David: Hi there, I'm here to check in for my flight.

Sally: OK, and where are you headed today, sir?

David: I'm flying to Chicago.

Sally: Perfect. I'll just need your passport and your flight confirmation number.

David: I've got them right here.

Sally: Thanks. And would you prefer a ❶ _____ or an ❷ _____ today?

David: I'll take the window.

Sally: Do you have any special ❸ _____ we should know about?

David: Nope, not for me.

Sally: How many ❹ _____ will you be checking in today, sir?

David: Just my suitcase.

Sally: OK, here is your boarding pass, passport and ❺ _____ sticker. Don't lose it. Oh, and you'll have to ❻ _____ in Detroit. Don't worry. You'll have plenty of time to make your ❼ _____ . Have a pleasant flight.

Words to Remember

Use the words in the box to complete the sentences.

window seat	aisle seat	meal preference	baggage claim
bag	transfer	connection	

1. Karen needed four _____ to carry all her stuff.

2. Ian's flight was delayed, so he missed his _____ .

3. Mark's flight landed in Los Angeles, and then he had to _____ to San Francisco.

4. Tammy likes to get a _____ so she can look at the clouds.

5. Greg said that his _____ was for the vegetarian meal.

Get It Right

Pretend you are David, and you are writing to Justin about your first experience at an airport. Write out what happened at the airport, and use at least three adverbs or adverbial phrases of time, place and frequency in the letter.

_____

_____

_____

_____

_____

Grammar Bite

When we have to go somewhere to do something, we have to use adverbs and adverbial phrases of time, place, and frequency. These describe when, where, and how often something happens. So you can see how useful adverbial phrases will be when describing something like going to the airport to catch a flight.

The following are some adverbs and adverbial phrases for each situation.

- **Time:**   every day, every week, twice a day, twice a month, all the time

- **Place:**   outside, inside, indoors, outdoors

- **Frequency:** always, sometimes, often, usually, never

Give It a Try

Choose which form of each sentence below is correct. Note: one of the options is a common mistake made by English learners when using adverbs and adverbial phrases of time, place, and frequency.

_____ **1. a.** I will take a flight next week.   **b.** I next week will take a flight.

_____ **2. a.** As a pilot, Jeff has to go to the airport every day.   **b.** As a pilot, Jeff has to go to the airport every days.

_____ **3. a.** I went yesterday to the airport.   **b.** Yesterday I went to the airport.

_____ **4. a.** I'm going now to the gate.   **b.** I'm going to the gate now.

_____ **5. a.** I have to change some money next.   **b.** I next have to change some money.

Prepare Yourself

Look at the pictures below. In them, you'll see various people doing things they would normally have to do in an airport.

lost luggage

working

security checking

duty free shopping

passport control

check-in

baggage claim

flight delay

Activity

With a partner, take turns answering the following questions about the pictures above.

1. Which of these processes of going through an airport is your least favorite and why?
2. What are some things you need to prepare before heading to the airport?
3. What might happen when you go through passport control?
4. What will happen just before you board the airplane?

Useful Expressions

- Before you go to the *airport* you need to have *all your travel documents*.
- When you go to *check in*, make sure you have your *passport* ready.
- After you *check in*, go to the *security screening checkpoint*.
- While you're waiting at the gate, *read a book* or *listen to music* to pass the time.

 Listening

Track 11 Listen to the conversation between George and Paulette. Are the statements about the conversation true or false?

1. Paulette likes traveling with a group.   True / False

2. George prefers to travel alone.   True / False

3. It's easier to meet locals when traveling alone.   True / False

4. George is considering traveling by himself next time.   True / False

5. Paulette and George will travel together.   True / False

 Vocabulary

Complete the conversation using the words in the box.

book	itinerary	guide book	transportation	forum

A: I'm so excited to ❶ _____ my next trip.

B: Where are you planning to go?

A: I want to go to Spain. I've been reading a ❷ _____ about the country, and it looks amazing.

B: You might want to check out an online ❸ _____ as well before you start making your plans. Travelers post some useful tips there for you to check out.

A: OK, I'll do that before I start writing up my ❹ _____.

B: Do you have any plans as far as local ❺ _____ yet? I mean, how are you planning to get from city to city?

A: I'll just take local buses. They're cheap and pretty reliable. It's going to be great!

 Grammar

Decide whether the underlined nouns in each of the following sentences are countable or uncountable.

1. The children are packing their <u>suitcases</u> for the trip   Countable / Uncountable

2. I put two small <u>bottles</u> of water in my bag, just in case.   Countable / Uncountable

3. Put your <u>luggage</u> in the car and then we'll go.   Countable / Uncountable

4. Did you remember to pack your favorite <u>shirt</u>?   Countable / Uncountable

5. There are so many people waiting for the <u>flight</u> to depart.   Countable / Uncountable

 Reading

Complete the words in the text. The first letters are given.

It happens to the best of us. You're on vacation, and you mis   something.
It could be something minor, like a shirt or a pair of shoes. Or it could be something very
imp   , like a passport or some other vital document. Travel often enough, and
chances are you'll lose at least one thing along the way. How do you avoid for
something in your hotel or hostel room? The best way to rem   everything is to
make a list. Write down everything you brought with you. Then, before you check out of your room,
go through that list of your st   . Check off each item as you see it. That way,
nothing will ever get left behind.

 Conversation

Match the sentences 1-5 with the correct responses a-e.

        1. Hi, I'm here to check in for my flight.

        2. Would you prefer a window or an aisle seat?

        3. Do you have a meal preference on your flight today?

        4. How many bags will you be checking in today?

        5. Will I have to transfer anywhere?

a I'm a vegetarian, so no meat, please.

b I'd like to be able to see outside, thanks.

c I just have one suitcase.

d No, your flight goes directly to your final destination.

e Where are you headed today?

Checking In / Out

By the end of this unit, you will be able to do the following:

→ Check in and check out of a hotel
→ Talk about services offered at a hotel
→ Give requests to the hotel receptionist
→ Discuss the details of a hotel bill

Before We Go

Look at the pictures below of a hotel. Match the numbered pictures (1-6) with the correct term in the box.

receptionist	*reception desk*	*bellhop*
luggage cart	*elevator*	*key card*

①   ②   ③

④   ⑤   ⑥

Useful Expressions

- Do you have a *reservation*?
- Could I see your *ID*, please?

- Can I have a wake-up call *tomorrow*?
- Do you have any *rooms* available?

Conversation 1

Track 12 Carrie is checking in to a hostel. She is at the reception desk, speaking with the receptionist. Listen to the conversation and fill in the missing words.

Carrie: Hello, I have a ❶ _____ under the name Carrie Ronald.

Receptionist: Let me check our records. Ah, here it is. Yes, you've ❷ _____ one bed in a shared dorm for two nights. Is that correct?

Carrie: Yes, and I read online that all your ❸ _____ have Wi-Fi. Is that right?

Receptionist: That's right. But just to let you know, we also have a business center located on the second ❹ _____. There are several computers there for our guests to use free of charge.

Carrie: Perfect.

Receptionist: How will you be paying today, Miss Ronald?

Carrie: Credit card.

Receptionist: Excellent. Your booking comes with a complimentary breakfast in our restaurant. Breakfast is served from six a.m. to 9 a.m. Unfortunately, we don't offer ❺ _____, but you're welcome to bring food back to your dorm.

Carrie: That's great. Could I get a ❻ _____ tomorrow?

Receptionist: Certainly, what time?

Carrie: 5:30 a.m. I like to work out early in the morning.

Receptionist: It's all arranged, Miss Ronald. Thank you, and enjoy your ❼ _____ with us. Here's your key card. One of our staff will help take your ❽ _____ to your room.

Words to Remember

Use the words in the box to complete the sentences.

floor	room	stay	book
reservation	room service	luggage	wake-up call

1. Jeremy made a _____ at the B&B.
2. What _____ is my room on?
3. Roger always _____ hotel rooms online.
4. We hope you have a pleasant _____ with us here at the Royal Oaks Inn.
5. I will require a _____ at 7 a.m. tomorrow.

🎈 Reading

🎧**Track 13** Read this announcement from the management of a hostel. It's about a few rules the hostel has for its guests.

Dear Guests,

Thank you for choosing to stay here with us at Happy Valley Hostel. We hope you'll enjoy your time here, and if there is anything we can do to make your stay more enjoyable, please don't hesitate to ask. After you get settled in, please take a moment to familiarize yourself with our house rules.

1. **No outside guests allowed in the rooms overnight. This is for your safety, as well as that of our other guests.**
2. **The front door will be locked each night at midnight. If you return after midnight, simply ring the bell at the door, and one of our staff will unlock it to let you in.**
3. **Please keep the kitchen clean. Our kitchen is free for all our guests to use if you wish to cook for yourself. However, please clean any dishes you use when you are finished.**
4. **After 10 p.m. is quiet time. Please avoid making any loud noises after this time. Some of our guests may already be asleep.**
5. **Please avoid monopolizing the laundry facilities. The laundry room is also free for our guests to use, but please avoid using the machines for too long. Other people wish to use them as well.**

Thank you for taking the time to read this over. If you have any questions or concerns, please feel free to bring them to our staff. Have a pleasant stay!

Sincerely,

The management

🎈 Give It a Try

Based on the announcement, choose the correct answer for the following questions.

1. What is the main purpose of the announcement?
   a. It tells where the kitchen is.
   b. It explains how to use a laundry machine.
   c. It introduces some guests.
   d. It explains some rules.

2. What happens each night at midnight?
   a. The front door is locked.
   b. Guests must leave.
   c. The kitchen is closed.
   d. The laundry room is opened.

3. What must guests do after 10 p.m.?
   a. Check in.
   b. Cook in the kitchen.
   c. Do their laundry.
   d. Keep quiet.

4. How much does it cost to use the laundry facilities?
   a. It is free only after midnight.
   b. The passage does not say.
   c. It is free.
   d. A few dollars.

5. What should guests remember about using the kitchen?
   a. Use it quickly.
   b. Keep it clean.
   c. Keep out.
   d. Never use it.

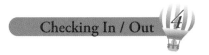

Conversation 2

Track 14 Carrie is now checking out of the hostel. She is discussing the bill with the receptionist. Listen to the conversation and fill in the missing words.

Carrie: Hi, I'm ❶ _____ .

Receptionist: Ah, Miss Ronald. Did you ❷ _____ your stay with us?

Carrie: Yes, very much. You've got a lovely establishment here.

Receptionist: That's great to hear. We welcome ❸ _____ from our guests, positive or negative. OK, I've got your ❹ _____ here. Please take a minute to look it over and make sure it's accurate.

Carrie: OK, let me see...what's this ❺ _____ here?

Receptionist: Oh, that's for the sightseeing tour we arranged for you the other day.

Carrie: Right, I remember you explained that you charged a small ❻ _____ for arranging it.

Receptionist: Also note that we've returned your security ❼ _____ .

Carrie: OK, I see that. Everything looks good to me.

Receptionist: Fantastic, I'll just print off your ❽ _____ . Are you heading for the airport?

Carrie: Yes, would it be possible for you to call a taxi for me?

Receptionist: Absolutely, we'll have one here for you shortly. We hope to see you again.

Words to Remember

Choose the words in the box to complete the following sentences.

charge	*check out*	*fee*	*receipt*
deposit	*enjoy*	*feedback*	*bill*

1. Ian _____ of the hotel at the end of his stay.

2. The cashier handed me a _____ after I paid.

3. You must pay a _____ , but it will be returned to you later.

4. We hope you _____ tonight's performance.

5. After the meal was over, James paid the _____ .

Get It Right

Pretend you are booking a hostel online. You are writing an e-mail to the management, and you are outlining a few requests that you have. Use *want / would like* constructions to communicate those requests to the management.

○○○

Hello,

My name is _____, and I have booked a room at your hostel for three days next week, starting Wednesday. I would like to see and do many things while I'm there. First of all, I want to arrange ...

_____

_____

_____

_____

Grammar Bite

Want / would like to do something is a common sentence construction that is used in the hospitality industry. It is used by both staff and guests alike to communicate things that they want to do, or require, or to inquire about those needs.

Remember, *would like* is similar in meaning to *want*, but it is considered more polite. *Would like* can be followed by a noun, or by *to + Verb*.

Examples:

* *Would* you *like* a wake-up call tomorrow morning?
* *Would* you *like* coffee with your meal?
* *Would* you *like* to go shopping?
* Do you *want* some ice cream?

Give It a Try

Choose which form of each sentence below is correct.

1. I would *(like to / like for to)* check in.

2. I would *(like / like to)* arrange a trip to the temple tomorrow.

3. *(You would like / Would you like)* something to eat?

4. *(He would like some tea. / Some tea he would like.)*

5. Jonathan would *(like to / like)* go to Japan.

Prepare Yourself

Look at the pictures below. In them, you'll see various items or services that would normally be provided in a hostel.

tour info

lockers

breakfast

washing machine

kitchen

reception

Activity 1

With a partner, take turns answering the following questions about the pictures above.

1. What is the man standing next to the reception desk doing?
2. What is happening in the hostel kitchen?
3. Where can guests go if they want to arrange a tour?
4. What services are offered at the hostel?

Activity 2

With a partner, act out a scene in which one of you is checking into a hostel, and the other is the receptionist. Then, switch roles and act out the scene once more.

Useful Expressions

- I'd like to *check in*.
- How long will you be *staying with us*?
- How would you like to *pay*?
- I'd like a *single / double room / shared dorm*.

Meeting Roommates

By the end of this unit, you will be able to do the following:

✈ Meet and greet new roommates
✈ Start up a conversation with someone you've never met before
✈ Ask questions and get basic information about people
✈ Converse easily with people from different backgrounds

Before We Go

Look at the pictures of a hostel dorm room below. Match the numbered items (1-5) with the correct term in the box.

| *bunk bed* | *closet* | *bathroom* | *nightstand* | *roommate* |

① _____

② _____

③ _____

④ _____

⑤ _____

Useful Expressions

- Hello, nice to meet you, my name is *Josh*.
- Where *are you* from?
- How long have you been *traveling*?
- What do you do *back home*?

Conversation 1

Track 15 Josh has just walked into a hostel dorm. He meets Dana, a fellow traveler. Listen to the conversation and fill in the missing words.

Josh: Hi there. Nice to meet you. My name is Josh. What's your name?

Dana: Hi, I'm Dana. Nice to meet you, too.

Josh: So, Dana, how long have you been ❶ _____?

Dana: Oh, I've been ❷ _____ for about six months. And you?

Josh: Almost a year. I've lost track of how many ❸ _____ rooms I've stayed in.

Dana: I'll bet. Don't you ever get tired of living out of ❹ _____ rooms?

Josh: Not really. I like ❺ _____ in new places all the time. What do you do ❻ _____, Dana?

Dana: I was working in a restaurant before I left. When I go back I'll probably do the same. My ❼ _____ is always asking when I'm going to come home and start working again.

Josh: Same here. But I understand where they're coming from. Do you have brothers and sisters?

Dana: One of each. ❽ _____?

Josh: Nope, I'm an only child.

Dana: Well, I guess you've got lots of new brothers and sisters from your time on the road.

Words to Remember

Choose the words in the box to complete the sentences.

travel	what about you	hostel	wake up
dorm	back home	family	on the road

1. Mark loves to _____ and see new places.

2. On his current trip, Travis has been _____ for eight months.

3. There were 12 people staying in the same _____ room, which had six bunk beds.

4. When meeting new people, ask about their _____, such as their brothers and sisters.

5. Maria isn't working while she travels, but _____ she was a dentist.

 # Reading

Track 16 Read this article about meeting new people when you check into a hostel.

Meeting new people when traveling isn't easy sometimes. It's hard to walk up to a total stranger and strike up a conversation. But there are some easy ways to introduce yourself when you first check into a hostel and start making new friends right away. When you arrive in your room, don't hesitate. If you're really quiet when you first get in, your roommates might just think you're the quiet type and want to be left alone. Introduce yourself right away. Try to be outgoing. If you take that first step, the ones that follow will be much easier.

Then, make sure you don't spend too much time talking about yourself. Ask questions about your fellow travelers and take an interest in their lives. They'll appreciate it much more than if you just carry on about what you've been doing. If you seem interested in them, they'll show an interest in you.

Also, be considerate of everyone in the dorm room. Try not to make loud noises early in the morning or late at night when others are still sleeping. And don't tie up the bathroom for too long. If you do, you might find your roommates leaving you behind when they go out for the day or night together. Don't be afraid to share, either. Travelers are always running out of this or that on the road. If one of your roommates needs something simple that you can part with, share it. You'll have a loyal friend for life. Keep these tips in mind and you'll be meeting new people in no time.

 # Give It a Try

Based on the article, choose the correct answer for the following questions.

1. What is the main idea of this passage?
   a. How to find a roommate.
   b. How to check in to a dorm.
   c. How to meet people.
   d. How to keep your privacy.

2. What should you do when you first enter a dorm room?
   a. Ask questions.
   b. Stay quiet.
   c. Unpack your stuff.
   d. Say hello.

3. What should you avoid doing in the early morning and late at night?
   a. Making friends
   b. Making noise
   c. Making food
   d. Making room

4. What should you do to show your interest in your fellow travelers?
   a. Say nothing at all.
   b. Say as little as possible.
   c. Talk about yourself.
   d. Ask questions about them.

5. Which of the following is a way to be considerate of everyone in your dorm room?
   a. Give away everything.
   b. Keep what's yours.
   c. Share what you have.
   d. Don't talk to anyone.

Conversation 2

Track 17 It's late in the evening, and Josh and his fellow travelers are getting ready to turn in. Listen to the conversation and fill in the missing words.

Josh: Hey Dana. What were you ❶ _____ today?

Dana: Oh, I just toured around the city by myself for a while. What about you?

Josh: I visited a couple of museums with some new friends. It's so easy to ❷ _____ people here.

Dana: Yeah, everybody seems very ❸ _____. My problem is I'm a bit ❹ _____. Maybe you could help me meet some of the other people here.

Josh: Sure, no problem. I've always been good at talking to new people. Say, is the bathroom ❺ _____? I want to brush my teeth.

Dana: I think so. One of the guys has been in there for 45 minutes.

Josh: Man, other people need to get in there too. That's just ❻ _____.

Dana: I think it's the same guy who was listening to loud music early this morning. He woke everyone up.

Josh: Oh, that was him? Someone should let him know he's being very rude to the other ❼ _____.

Dana: Maybe you could do it. He seems to be having trouble ❽ _____ everyone.

Josh: I'll just have a polite word with him. If he ever gets out of the bathroom, that is.

Dana: All part of staying in a hostel dorm, I guess.

Words to Remember

Choose the words in the box to complete the following sentences.

up to	meet	friendly	shy
occupied	selfish	guest	get along with

1. Karina is very _____, so she has no trouble making new friends.
2. My friend is asking me what I am _____ today.
3. There are four _____ staying in this room tonight.
4. I think James is difficult to _____ early in the morning.
5. Tammy is _____, so she has trouble speaking to people she doesn't know.

 Get It Right

Pretend you are introducing yourself to someone at a hostel for the first time. Write out what you would say to that person, and what details you would reveal to them. Use the Present Perfect tense.

Hi, I'm _____ . What's your name? I've been traveling for six months. I've actually been to this city before. It is my second time here...

_____

_____

_____

_____

_____

 Grammar Bite

The Present Perfect tense is often used in conversations where we're meeting people for the first time. It is used to describe things that happened in the past and are still true now because you can see the result. It is also used to describe experiences you've had in your life.

Lastly, the Present Perfect tense is used to describe events that started in the past and are still happening now. The tense is formed as:

Subject + have / has + Present Perfect Verb

Examples:

- I've *watched* this TV show before.
- Tracy *has played* this game many times.
- They *have read* this book twice.

 Give It a Try

Choose which form of each pair of sentences below is the correct usage of the Present Perfect tense.

1. *(I've lived here for / I lived here)* my whole life.
2. *(I saw / I've seen)* this movie twice.
3. *(I've been to / I go to)* Berlin three times.
4. *(I've twisted / I twisted)* my ankle yesterday.
5. Jeffrey *(has been / went)* to Prague last week.

Prepare Yourself

Look at the pictures below of people mingling in a hostel.

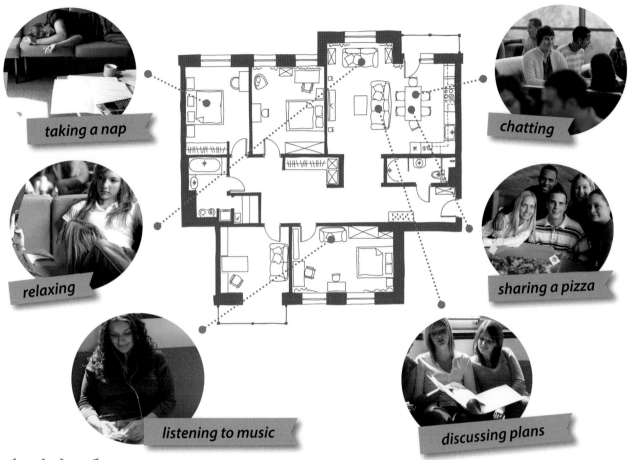

taking a nap

chatting

relaxing

sharing a pizza

listening to music

discussing plans

Activity 1

With a partner, take turns answering the following questions about the pictures above.

1. What is the best way to introduce yourself to someone for the first time?

2. If there's someone you don't get along with in your dorm, how should you handle it?

3. What are the most important things to remember when living in a dorm?

4. What are the best and worst parts about hostel dorm life and having roommates?

Activity 2

With a partner, act out a scene in which both of you are travelers meeting for the first time in a hostel. Ask each other questions about your lives, and find out as much as you can about each other.

Useful Expressions

- It's great to meet *you*.
- How *are you* doing?
- What *are your* favorite things to do?
- Tell me about *your family*.

Unit 6

Housekeeping

By the end of this unit, you will be able to do the following:

→ Ask for and describe different cleaning supplies
→ Talk about cleaning up a room
→ Ask people for assistance when cleaning
→ Give cleaning instructions to others

Before We Go

Look at the pictures of various cleaning supplies below. Match the numbered items (1-6) with the correct term in the box.

| scrub | brush | glass cleaner fluid | rag | dustpan | broom |

① ② ③

④ ⑤

⑥

Useful Expressions

- Can you pass me the *broom*, please?
- I'll get started on the *bathroom*. You can *make the beds*.

- Be sure to *give the floor a good scrubbing*.
- Spray some cleaning solution on the *table* and wipe it off.

Conversation 1

Track 18 It's time to do a little cleaning in the hostel dorm room. Tina and one of her roommates, Darren, are about to get to work. Listen to the conversation and fill in the missing words.

Tina: Well, this room isn't going to ❶ _____ itself. We'd better get started.

Darren: OK, what should we do first?

Tina: I'll ❷ _____ the shelves. If you don't mind, you can ❸ _____ the floor.

Darren: Sure, I can handle that. What else do we have to do?

Tina: The floor could probably use a good ❹ _____ as well.

Darren: I'll ask one of our other roommates to do that. What about the bathroom?

Tina: Oh, right. I almost forgot. I think the toilet needs to be ❺ _____ .

Darren: Gross, I'll definitely get someone else to do that.

Tina: I think the drain in the sink is ❻ _____ , too. I think there's some clog remover somewhere in there.

Darren: There are some dirty dishes in the kitchen as well. Someone will have to wash those.

Tina: They've been sitting there a while. ❼ _____ them first.

Darren: And then there's the ❽ _____ to do. We sure have a busy day ahead of us.

Words to Remember

Choose the words in the box to complete the sentences.

laundry	sweep	soak	mop
scrub	clean	clog	dust

1. The dirty clothes are piling up, so I'd better do the _____ .

2. Wanda left the dirty dishes to _____ in some soapy water.

3. There's dust on the floor, so you need to _____ it.

4. Please _____ the bathtub, as it's very dirty.

5. The water in the sink won't go down. I think it might be _____ .

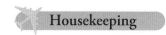

 Reading

Track 19 Read this article about dividing up cleaning chores fairly among roommates.

Having roommates is great, except when it comes to cleaning. We've all had that one roommate who simply refuses to do his or her share of the housework. It can become a real pain if the other people staying in the dorm room have to do everything for that one person who doesn't pull their own weight. But there is a fair way to divide up the housework. One way is to make it completely random. Draw straws to see who has to do what. Or write down all the chores on little bits of paper, and then have each roommate pick a piece of paper out of a hat. It can add a bit of fun to something that's not fun at all.

If you have roommates that you're going to be staying with for a while, you might consider making a list, and rotating all the different chores through each of your roommates. One week is your week to clean the bathroom, and the next week that job passes to one of your other roommates. Eventually, the job comes back to you. It's fair, and no one has to do a job they don't like doing more than anyone else. Another way is to make all of the cleaning the responsibility of one roommate for one whole week. One week it's your week to clean everything, and the next week that job passes to the next person. Of course, that makes for a busy week. But on the plus side, it means once your cleaning week is over, it's a long time before you have to clean again. Try these out, and hopefully cleaning problems will be a thing of the past while you're on the road.

 Give It a Try

Based on the article, choose the correct answer for the following questions.

1. What is the main purpose of this passage?
   a. To show that cleaning is never fun
   b. To teach you how to clean your bathroom
   c. To talk about living with roommates
   d. To give tips on cleaning chores

2. In what way can you make sure it will be a long time before you have to clean again?
   a. Draw chores out of a hat
   b. Make cleaning a week-long responsibility
   c. Make a list of chores
   d. Draw straws for cleaning chores

3. What is true of making a list of chores for everyone?
   a. It ensures the cleaning won't get done.
   b. It's a way to make cleaning more complicated.
   c. It's a strange idea.
   d. It's a fair method.

4. Which of the following statements is true, according to the passage?
   a. Drawing straws for chores is not fun.
   b. There's always one roommate who doesn't clean.
   c. When cleaning, you must wear a hat.
   d. Every roommate always pulls their weight.

5. If you don't want to do a job you don't like more than anyone else, you should do which of the following?
   a. Make a list
   b. Draw chores from a hat
   c. Divide cleaning up on a weekly basis
   d. Get new roommates

Conversation 2

 Track 20 Ted and his hostel roommates have run out of cleaning supplies. So, Ted goes to the store to pick some up. He is talking to Samantha, who works in the store. Listen to the conversation and fill in the missing words.

Ted: Hi, I'm running low on a few things. Could you help me out?

Samantha: Sure, what do you need?

Ted: We've been washing our clothes in the ❶ _____ at our hostel, but our clothes keep coming out a bit stiff. What do you recommend?

Samantha: Here, try out this ❷ _____. Just throw one sheet in the ❸ _____ with your clothes and they'll come out soft and fluffy.

Ted: Great. We also need something for our bathroom window. It's so dirty we can't see our faces in it anymore.

Samantha: We have a sale on this glass ❹ _____. That should do the trick.

Ted: Then there's the carpet. We've spilled some food and drinks on it.

Samantha: Try out this ❺ _____. It removes everything from small spots to large ❻ _____.

Ted: That's perfect. Oh, and one more thing about our clothes. Some of them have stains that we can't seem to get out.

Samantha: Hmm, they might need to be ❼ _____. I'm afraid we can't help you out on that one.

Ted: No problem. Well, I think that's everything. Any more tips?

Samantha: Yeah, maybe you should just hire a ❽ _____.

Words to Remember

Choose the words in the box to complete the following sentences.

stain	*dry clean*	*dryer*	*maid*
spot remover	*washing machine*	*fabric softener*	*cleaning solution*

1. Put those dirty clothes in the _____.
2. There is a big _____ on the carpet. Did you spill a drink in here?
3. The _____ comes once a week to clean the house.
4. These clothes can't be washed in the machine, so you'll have to take them to be _____.
5. It's been raining for weeks and I have to use a _____ for my laundry.

Get It Right

Pretend you are leaving some cleaning instructions for your roommates. Write out what you want each of them to do. Use a form of "be going to" at least three times.

Hi everyone, today we're going to clean up the room. Here is the job for everyone:

1.   I am going to clean the kitchen sink.
2.   Tony is going to wash the windows.
3. _____
4. _____

 Grammar Bite

Be going to is a common phrase in English that we use to express what we are going to do in the future. We can also use it to express what are not going to do. It's useful when talking about cleaning up, but make sure the singular form of the verb be goes with a singular noun. The plural form of "be" goes with a plural noun, or when there is more than one subject. Another common mistake people make is that they forget to add the verb "be" before "going to".

I / you / we / they	+	are going to
He / she / it		is going to

Examples:

- Today we *are going to* clean the house.
- They *are going to* fix the car.
- He *is going to* watch TV.

Give It a Try

Choose which form of each sentence below is the correct usage of the phrase "be going to".

1. Paul and Jackson *(are / is)* going to clean the living room.

2. Nancy *(is / are)* going to mop the floor.

3. I *(going to / am going to)* vacuum the rug.

4. A: Are Jenny and Alice going to wash the bathroom?

   B: Yes, they *(going to / are going to)* wash the dishes.

5. A: Are you going to do the laundry?

   B: No, I *(is not / am not)* going to do the laundry. I'm going to take a nap.

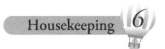

Prepare Yourself

Look at the pictures below of roommates cleaning up a room in a hostel.

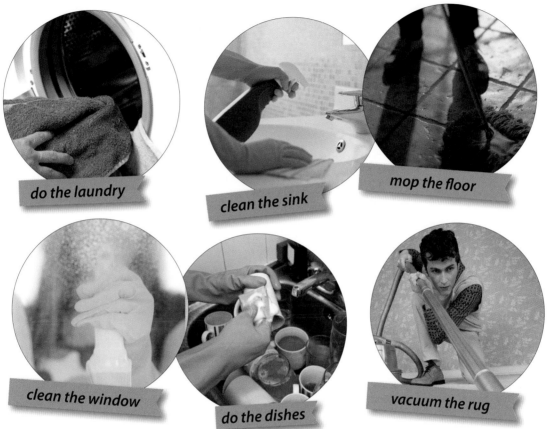

do the laundry

clean the sink

mop the floor

clean the window

do the dishes

vacuum the rug

Activity 1

With a partner, take turns answering the following questions about the pictures above.

1. If you had to pick one, which cleaning job taking place in the pictures would you pick and why?
2. What is the easiest cleaning job taking place in the pictures?
3. What is your favorite and least favorite cleaning job?
4. Do you enjoy cleaning? Why or why not?

Activity 2

With a partner, you are going to act out a scene. In the scene, one of you is in charge of dividing up the cleaning chores. That person will explain to the other what they will have to clean, and how they should do it. Act out the scene once, and then switch roles and do it one more time.

Useful Expressions

- You can start by *taking out the trash*.
- Then, move on to the *living room*.
- Don't forget to *vacuum the carpet*.
- Once you've *mopped the floor*, you'll have to dry it.

Listening

Track 21 **Listen and number the events which take place during the conversation in order.**

     Peter inquires about using the Internet.

     Peter pays for his room.

     Peter tells the clerk his payment method.

     The clerk changes Peter's room booking.

     The clerk writes down the password.

     The clerk tells Peter he is early.

Vocabulary

Complete the sentences with the words in the box.

meet	friendly	shy	wake up	guest

1. I love staying in hostels because it's so easy to _____ people.

2. David is very _____, so he finds it difficult to talk to people when traveling.

3. Everyone here is so _____. I can't believe how nice everyone is.

4. There aren't many _____ in this hostel. It must be low season.

5. What time do you usually _____ in the morning?

Grammar

Choose which form of each pair of sentences below is the correct usage of the Present Perfect tense.

1. *(I've been to / I go to)* Rome twice.

2. John *(has been to Venice. / has been to Venice last week)*.

3. I've lived in New York *(for my whole life. / my whole life.)*

Reading

Fill in the blanks with the correct word. The first letters are already given.

The other day, I went down to the laundry room at my hostel. I put my clothes in the

was _____ machine. But when I took them out, they were stiff. So I went down to

the store to get some fa _____ softener. While I was there, I decided to pick up a

few more supplies. I had noticed that the bathroom window was really dirty, so I bought some cleaning

sol _____. And in the guest lounge, someone had spilled food and drinks on the carpet. I

hope the sp _____ remover I purchased will get those st _____ out. It

looks like I'll be busy cleaning up the hostel for a while.

Conversation

Choose the correct words to complete the conversation.

A: Our room is so dirty.

B: Well, it's not going to clean *(itself / ourselves)*. Let's get busy.

A: I'll *(dust / mop)* the shelves.

B: OK, and I'll *(scrub / sweep)* the toilet.

A: Someone will also have to *(clog / wash)* the dishes.

B: I'll ask Steve if he can help with that.

Unit 7

Buying Groceries

By the end of this unit, you will be able to do the following:

✈ Shop for groceries in a foreign country
✈ Convert prices from the local currency to your own
✈ Ask for help finding specific items in a grocery store
✈ Make a budget for buying groceries

Before We Go

Look at the pictures of these common items we might buy at a grocery store. Match the numbered items (1-6) with the correct term in the box.

| cereal | vegetables | meat | milk | bread | fruit |

① _____ ② _____ ③ _____

④ _____ ⑤ _____ ⑥ _____

Useful Expressions

• We're out of *milk*, so we'll need to buy some.
• We can't afford *this steak*. It's not in our budget.

• The *produce* is in aisle three.
• I'm not sure if we need *potatoes*. Let me check the list.

Conversation 1

Track 22 Miranda and one of her roommates, Tyler, are running low on food. So, they've come to a local grocery store to purchase a few things. Listen to the conversation and fill in the missing words.

Miranda: What do we need to ❶ _____ today?

Tyler: I've got all the ❷ _____ written down on our ❸ _____.

Miranda: Oh, first of all, I'll get us a ❹ _____.

Tyler: OK, but we can't buy too much. We have to stay within our ❺ _____.

Miranda: How did you come up with a budget?

Tyler: I have a limit on how much I can spend each week while I'm traveling. I put about 12 percent of that weekly amount towards food.

Miranda: That's a good tip. So, what's first on our list?

Tyler: We need some healthy fruits and vegetables. Oh, I see them there. But the prices are all in euros. How do we ❻ _____ that to dollars?

Miranda: One U.S. dollar is equal to about €0.75 at the current ❼ _____.

Tyler: All right. We can only spend about €40, between the two of us.

Miranda: That's a tight budget. Let's head to the frozen foods ❽ _____ There should be some ❾ _____ over there.

Tyler: Good thinking. Hopefully we can save some cash.

Words to Remember

Choose the words in the box to complete the sentences.

convert	deal	item	budget	exchange rate
pick up	list	cart	section	

1. If you need to _____ currency, check the exchange rate first.

2. You'll find milk in the dairy _____ of the grocery store.

3. Graham has a food _____ of 50 dollars a week.

4. Wayne went to the store to _____ some food.

5. If you look for special _____, sometimes you can save a lot of money.

 # Reading

Track 23 **Read this article about preparing a food budget.**

One of the skills every traveler needs is the ability to manage their money wisely. One of the toughest things to budget for is food. It's hard to determine exactly how much you should spend on it. With that being said, there are a few simple things everyone can do to make sure their food budget doesn't get out of control. First of all, you need to know how much you're comfortable spending each month. Once you know that, you can break down that figure into categories such as entertainment, transportation, and food. What percentage should go towards food? Experts recommend spending anywhere from 9 to 14 percent of your monthly income on food. So, take what you're comfortable spending, and calculate about 10 percent of that. That will be your food budget for the month.

The hard part will be sticking to that budget. Try to buy groceries whenever possible and cook for yourself. In the long run, it's much cheaper than eating out all the time. Don't splurge on things you don't really need, either. Stick to the basics, and leave the sweets and other unnecessary products alone. A treat once in a while is fine, but don't make it a habit. If this is difficult for you, try to look at everything you buy in terms of the number of days you can travel. If you buy something you don't really need, it takes away from your travel time. So make a budget, stick to it, and keep traveling for as long as you can.

 # Give It a Try

Based on the article, choose the correct answer for the following questions.

1. What is the main purpose of this passage?
   a. To show you how to prepare a food budget
   b. To tell you what restaurants to eat at
   c. To show which foods are healthy or unhealthy
   d. To tell you not to eat sweets

2. What percentage of your overall budget should go towards food, according to the passage?
   a. Less than nine percent
   b. Nine percent
   c. Between nine and fourteen percent
   d. Fourteen percent

3. Which of the following things is recommended in the article?
   a. Don't worry about how much you'll spend.
   b. Think of traveling in terms of how many meals you can buy.
   c. Purchase things you don't need.
   d. Buy groceries rather than eating out.

4. Which of the following things is difficult, according to the passage?
   a. Calculating percentages
   b. Finding a grocery store
   c. Sticking to a budget
   d. Buying groceries

5. Which of the following statements is true?
   a. Restaurants sell the cheapest basic items.
   b. Only buy sweets if they are cheap.
   c. A standard restaurant tip is 14 percent.
   d. Only buy basic items in the grocery store.

Conversation 2

Track 24 Miranda and Tyler have found everything they need. They are now ready to check out. They are chatting with the cashier as she rings up their items. Listen to the conversation and fill in the missing words.

Clerk: Did you ❶ _____ everything you were looking for today?

Tyler: Actually, there was one thing we couldn't find. Could you tell me where the cheddar cheese is? We looked all over the dairy section.

Clerk: Oh, actually that is ❷ _____ right now. We're expecting a ❸ _____ this afternoon.

Tyler: No problem, we can pick that up another time.

Clerk: These granola bars you've got are actually ❹ _____, two-for-one. Would you like to get another box?

Miranda: Sure, that sounds great. What's our ❺ _____?

Clerk: Your total comes to €38. Will that be cash, check, or credit card?

Miranda: We'll pay cash.

Tyler: We actually came in under budget. That's fantastic.

Miranda: We can put that two euros towards our food ❻ _____ for next week. We can use whatever we save to give ourselves a bit of breathing room.

Clerk: Do you need a ❼ _____ for your things?

Tyler: That's OK. We have our own reusable cloth bag for ❽ _____. It's better for the environment. Thanks!

Words to Remember

Choose the words in the box to complete the following sentences.

on sale	find	expense	delivery
out of stock	total	bag	grocery

1. This product is cheaper because it is _____.
2. I can't _____ the bread. Do you know where it is?
3. Your _____ comes to 27 dollars.
4. Please help me carry the _____ of groceries inside.
5. There isn't any milk on the shelves. It must be temporarily _____.

Get It Right

Pretend you are leaving a set of written instructions for your roommates to pick up the groceries you all need for the week. Divide up the items you need to get among your roommates, and make requests or tell them what to do using *can / could*. If need be, you can also use the negative forms, *can't / cannot*, or *couldn't / could not*.

Hi everyone,

I'm sorry I can't go with you to the grocery store today. But I've written out a list of everything we need. If everyone pitches in, it will go very quickly. Sally, you'll be in charge of picking up the dairy products. Could you get some milk and cheese? …

_____

_____

_____

_____

Grammar Bite

The modals *can* and *could* are used in a number of different situations. They are used to talk about your abilities at the present time. They are also used to make requests, with *could* being the more polite of the two. They can also be used to reply to those same requests, but remember, don't use *could* in replies to requests.

Another thing to remember is that there is always a verb after *can* and *could*, and the verb is always in the infinitive form. *Can / could* are useful when we go grocery shopping with our roommates on the road, because we might have to ask them to do something.

Examples:

- I'll go get some milk. *Could* you pick up a few vegetables?
- *Could* you come over here?
- I *can* do the job.
- *Could* you carry these bags for me?

Give It a Try

Choose which form of each sentence below is the correct usage of the positive or negative forms of the modals *can* and *could*.

1. *(You can / Can you)* speak English?
2. *(I could / Could I)* go with you?
3. I can *(go / to go)* grocery shopping with you.
4. A: Could you share the cost of the groceries?

   B: Yes, *(I can / I could)*.
5. Rhonda can go *(get / gets)* some fruit.

Prepare Yourself

Look at the pictures below of a bunch of groceries some hostel roommates have just purchased.

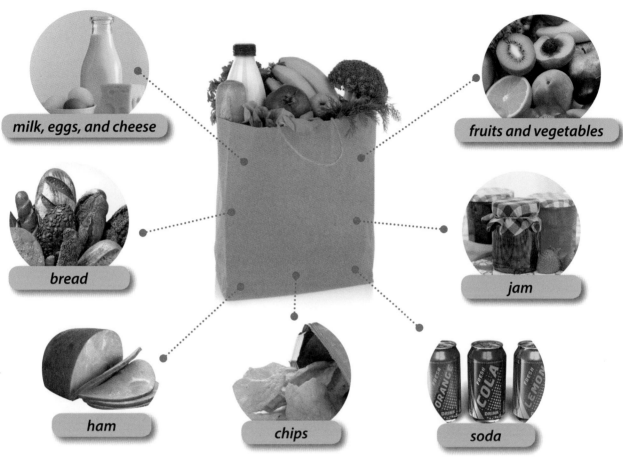

milk, eggs, and cheese

fruits and vegetables

bread

jam

ham

chips

soda

Activity 1

With a partner, take turns answering the following questions about the pictures above.

1. Do you enjoy going grocery shopping? Why or why not?
2. What sorts of things do you normally buy when you go to the grocery store?
3. What are some challenges involved in buying groceries in a foreign country?
4. How can going grocery shopping with roommates make it easier?

Activity 2

With a partner, act out a scene in which you are in a grocery store. Talk about what you would like to buy. You can also discuss your budget, and whether or not you can afford certain items. Act out the scene twice, with each of you taking turns being the one in charge of the budget.

Useful Expressions

- I don't think we can afford *this*.
- This is *within* our budget.
- Should we pick up some *grapes*?
- *Chips* are really a necessity.

Eating at a Market

By the end of this unit, you will be able to do the following:
→ Successfully navigate through a farmers market or traditional market
→ Identify different produce
→ Describe different tastes
→ Have an in-depth conversation about food

 ## Before We Go

Look at the pictures of these common foods and drinks we might find at a traditional market, or farmers market. Match the numbered items (1-10) with the correct term in the box.

potatoes	onions	meringue	apples	cheese
olives	spices	sweets	cherries	nuts

❶ ❷ ❸ ❹ ❺ ❻ ❼ ❽ ❾ ❿

Useful Expressions

- I'm going to get *a bag of chestnuts* from this *stall / vendor*.
- I'm in the mood for something *salty*.

- Let's see what the other *vendors* have to offer.
- I'm going to see if I can *haggle for a better price*.

Conversation 1

Track 25 Mike and Wanda are walking around a farmers market, trying to decide what they should get. Listen to the conversation and fill in the missing words.

Mike: So many ❶ _____ have set up shop here.

Wanda: Yeah, they come to the park every ❷ _____. What do you think we should try first?

Mike: There's no better place to get some fresh fruit. What's ❸ _____ now?

Wanda: ❹ _____, I think. Let's get some of those.

Mike: OK, and how about vegetables?

Wanda: I see a guy selling ❺ _____ over there. Those look tasty.

Mike: And that booth has heads of ❻ _____, and they're pretty cheap.

Wanda: There are some real ❼ _____ to be found.

Mike: Let's just take a walk around the whole thing first, then decide what to buy.

Wanda: That sounds like a plan.

Mike: Otherwise, we might end up coming home with a month's worth of food.

Wanda: We just need enough for a few days, so we'll have to be ❽ _____.

Words to Remember

Choose the words in the box to complete the sentences.

weekend	selective	mushroom	in season
bargain	farmer	strawberry	lettuce

1. My parents are _____. They grow wheat.

2. Jeremy prefers sweet fruits such as _____.

3. _____ is a vegetable used in many dishes.

4. Apples aren't available because they're not _____.

5. Everything in this store is so cheap. There are so many _____!

55

 Reading

Track 26 **Read this article about modern farmers markets.**

A farmers market is a very old concept, but it's something that disappeared for a while. A long time ago, everyone bought their meat, vegetables, and cheese at a farmers market. The market would be open every day, and that's where everyone bought their food. Then, in the 20th century, supermarkets emerged. Suddenly, people didn't need to buy their food directly from the source anymore. Instead of going to one person to get their meat, another for their dairy products, and so on, everything was available to them from one seller at the supermarket.

Today, farmers markets are making a big comeback. The reason is largely environmental. Food in supermarkets has to be shipped over large distances. This means fuel has to be used for trucks, trains, and airplanes, and that's bad for the environment. Food at the farmers market, on the other hand, comes from nearby. It might even come from your neighbor. Many people have also grown distrustful of large food companies. They don't know what chemicals they treat their products with, and so on. But at farmers markets, buyers have the chance to develop a personal relationship with the vendor they're buying from each and every week. They know how the food is grown or raised, and trust the person behind it. That's why more and more people are skipping the supermarket, and heading to the farmers market instead.

Give It a Try

Based on the article, choose the correct answer for the following questions.

1. What is the main purpose of this passage?
   a. It proves that supermarkets are superior.
   b. It explains why farmers markets are popular.
   c. It tells why people want to become farmers.
   d. It shows why farmers markets are struggling.

2. Why is food sold at farmers markets environmentally friendly, according to the article?
   a. Because it is not shipped from far away.
   b. Because it has lots of chemicals in it.
   c. Because it is bought at a supermarket.
   d. Because it is flown in an airplane.

3. Why do some people not trust large food companies?
   a. Because the companies might go out of business.
   b. Because they don't use enough chemicals.
   c. Because they don't know how their food is made.
   d. Because the companies don't pay fair wages.

4. What was true long ago, according to the article?
   a. There were no farmers markets long ago.
   b. Everyone bought their food at a supermarket.
   c. Farmers sold their food to supermarkets.
   d. Everyone bought their food at a farmers market.

5. What does the article imply?
   a. All food should be treated with chemicals.
   b. Supermarket chains will buy all of the farmers markets.
   c. More people are starting to shop at farmers markets.
   d. Farmers markets will soon be a thing of the past.

 # Conversation 2

Track 27 Mike and Wanda are now walking from stall to stall in the farmers market. They are discussing the different tastes of the various foods they come across. Listen to the conversation and fill in the missing words.

Mike: Check out this stall. A husband and wife are selling all different kinds of peppers.

Wanda: Those red ones look pretty ❶ _____. I can't really handle hot food.

Mike: I love spicy food. I put hot peppers on everything. Or what about that stall over there?

Wanda: Oh, the one selling ❷ _____ squash? I like bitter foods once in a while. They're usually pretty good for you.

Mike: Check this out. Here's a stall selling hot and ❸ _____ soup that's homemade using only ❹ _____ ingredients.

Wanda: I've actually had that before. It's ❺ _____. I enjoy it a lot. I might get a bowl later.

Mike: What about dessert?

Wanda: There's a stall on the other side of the market that sells cookies. They're ❻ _____, not too soft.

Mike: But I bought some cookies from them the other day, and they were ❼ _____. I think they weren't fresh.

Wanda: That's too bad. We could always get a donut instead. They're deep fried.

Mike: I'm not a big fan of ❽ _____ food. Deep fried foods are literally swimming in oil.

Wanda: OK, maybe we can give the cookies a second chance then.

Words to Remember

Choose the words in the box to complete the following sentences.

bitter	organic	oily	stale
tangy	spicy	crunchy	sour

1. Bill's food was so _____ he actually started to sweat.

2. Squeeze lemon over the fish to give it a _____ flavor.

3. I prefer _____ foods because there are no artificial chemicals in them.

4. Don't leave the bread on the counter or it will become _____.

5. _____ foods usually aren't healthy.

 # Get It Right

People often use the comparative form to show how foods are different from each other.

Example: I like the cookies at this stall better than the ones sold over there. They are much crunchier.

Your Turn: Write an e-mail to a friend describing your recent trip to a farmers market. In the e-mail, compare a few different stalls at the market which sell similar products. For example, you might compare one vegetable seller to another. Use the comparative form to describe a few different kinds of food, and give advice to your friend about where they should buy things when they visit the farmers market.

_____

_____

_____

_____

 # Grammar Bite

We use the comparative form to talk about how two things are different from each other.

There are some rules to follow when using comparative adjectives. If an adjective has one syllable, add *er* to the end.

If the adjective is two or more syllables, don't add *-er*; put *more* after *the*.

If the adjective already ends in *e*, just add *r*. If an adjective ends in one vowel and one consonant, write the consonant again, then write *er*. But never write a *w* twice. If an adjective has two syllables and ends in *y*, change the *y* to *i* and add *er*.

There are also adjectives that have irregular comparative forms, such as *good / better, bad / worse, far / further*.

Examples:

- Harry is *shorter than* Sally.
- Bob is *stronger than* Sam.
- Tina is *happier than* Susan.
- Mark's English is *worse than* Alex's.

 # Give It a Try

Change the following adjectives to their comparative form.

Adjectives	tall	thin		funny		happy	spicy	useful
Comparative			bigger		saltier			

Prepare Yourself

Look at the pictures below of various items that are commonly sold at a farmers market.

ham and sausages

produce

flowers

fish

cheese

cookies

Activity 1

With a partner, take turns answering the following questions about the pictures above.

1. What are the advantages of shopping at a farmers market?
2. Why should travelers buy their food at a farmers market?
3. What would a typical day for a farmer working at a farmers market be like?
4. What kind of people are you likely to meet at a farmers market?

Activity 2

Design a map of a farmers market, showing where all the different stalls are located. Take notes about which stalls you would want to visit, and what you would buy from them. In addition, take notes about what the food in each stall that you would visit tastes like. Share your plan with a partner, and then have your partner share his or her plan with you.

Useful Expressions

- First, I would visit the *vegetable stand* to get some *cucumbers*.
- I like *spicy dishes*, so I'd have to pick up some *peppers*.
- Next, I'd head for the *fruit stand* for some *apples*. They're a little bit *sweet*.
- Finally, I'd go to the *bakery* for some *fresh bread*. It's soft and *delicious*.

Unit 9

Eating at a Coffee Shop

By the end of this unit, you will be able to do the following:
→ Confidently place an order at a coffee shop
→ Read and understand a coffee shop menu
→ Have a conversation about different kinds of coffee on a menu
→ Discuss the daily specials or offers with a coffee shop clerk

Before We Go

Look at the pictures of these common foods and drinks we might order at a coffee shop. Match the numbered items (1-6) with the correct term in the box.

| donut | sandwich | muffin | croissant | coffee | tea |

① _____
② _____
③ _____
④ _____
⑤ _____
⑥ _____

Useful Expressions

- What would you like today?
- I'll have *a ham and cheese sandwich and a large black coffee*, please.
- Would you like anything else?
- Your total comes to *$4.75*.

Conversation 1

Track 28 Paul has walked into a coffee shop and is at the counter, ready to place his order. He is speaking to the clerk. Listen to the conversation and fill in the missing words.

Clerk: Hello, what can I get you today?

Paul: What's your lunch ❶ _____ today?

Clerk: Today we have a ❷ _____ and sandwich deal. It comes with a side ❸ _____ and your choice of coffee or tea.

Paul: That sounds good. I'll get that. For the sandwich I'll have the ham on rye bread. And what's your soup today?

Clerk: You can ❹ _____ between chicken noodle and cream of mushroom.

Paul: I'll ❺ _____ the cream of mushroom.

Clerk: OK, ❻ _____?

Paul: Oh, and could I get a large coffee ❼ _____, please? My roommate asked me to pick one up.

Clerk: Certainly. Your total comes to $9.50.

Paul: Here's ten.

Clerk: And 50 cents is your ❽ _____. Have a nice day.

Paul: You, too.

Words to Remember

Choose the words in the box to complete the sentences.

to go	*soup*	*special*	*choose*
go with	*salad*	*change*	*anything else*

1. Thomas was in a hurry, so he ordered his meal _____.

2. After looking at the menu a while, Frank decided to _____ a hamburger.

3. Wanting something healthy to eat, Harriet ordered a _____.

4. I'll get the daily _____ because it's a bit cheaper.

5. I don't know what to order. What will you _____?

Reading

Track 29 **Read this article about fair trade coffee shops.**

Have you ever thought about where your coffee comes from? These days, it's easier than ever to get a cup of coffee. There are coffee shops on every corner in cities around the world. But sadly there are some coffee companies which don't treat their workers well, or pay them a fair wage. So, the next time you need a cup of joe, look for a fair trade coffee shop. Fair trade coffee shops only buy their coffee beans or products from companies which are known to treat their workers fairly and pay them a decent wage. This movement grew when it started to become widely known that people working on large-scale coffee plantations, mostly in Third World countries, were being mistreated. Some people didn't feel comfortable ordering a cup of coffee knowing that the people who helped put it in their hands had to suffer. And so, they decided to do something about it.

Since the late 1980s, an international system of fair trade certification, known as "Fairtrade," has been in place. This means that not just any shop can say they practice fair trade. They have to meet certain standards before they do that. These standards are closely monitored by third parties, and if a product meets them, then the widely recognized Fairtrade logo can be placed on them. There are now coffee shops that only sell Fairtrade products. Sometimes these products are more expensive. The costs in producing them are higher, because workers are actually paid fairly. But the extra money you might pay is worth the peace of mind you get, knowing that nobody had to suffer for your morning cup of coffee.

Give It a Try

Based on the article, choose the correct answer for the following questions.

1. What is the main purpose of this passage?
   - **a.** To talk about a good cause
   - **b.** To tell you where the best coffee is
   - **c.** To discuss Third World politics
   - **d.** To explain why coffee is expensive

2. What is true about coffee shops, according to the article?
   - **a.** They are losing money.
   - **b.** They are disappearing.
   - **c.** They are raising their prices.
   - **d.** They are easy to find.

3. What does fair trade ensure?
   - **a.** Workers are treated well.
   - **b.** Workers can all get a cup of coffee.
   - **c.** Workers can keep their jobs.
   - **d.** Workers will suffer.

4. What must be true of a product that has the Fairtrade logo on it?
   - **a.** It is widely recognized by people.
   - **b.** It is less expensive than other similar products.
   - **c.** It has met certain standards.
   - **d.** It is only available in Third World countries.

5. What can buying fair trade coffee do for you, according to the article?
   - **a.** It can complicate your life.
   - **b.** It can increase your profits.
   - **c.** It can ease your mind
   - **d.** It can save you money.

Conversation 2

Track 30 Paul is walking down the street with Brenna, a fellow traveler. They stop in front of a coffee shop, which has a menu on display outside. Listen to the conversation and fill in the missing words.

Paul: I could go for a cup of coffee. How about you?

Brenna: Sure, but there are so many different kinds of coffee. I never know what to order.

Paul: Well, I usually keep things simple and order an
❶ _____ . It's just hot water and
❷ _____ .

Brenna: What's espresso?

Paul: It's a strong kind of coffee. It has a lot of caffeine. That's the stuff that gives you a quick
❸ _____ of energy.

Brenna: Oh, I don't want too much of that. It keeps me awake at night.

Paul: Then maybe you should order a
❹ _____ coffee, or decaf. It's coffee without the caffeine.

Brenna: It's only noon now. I think I can handle a real cup of coffee. What else do they have?

Paul: You could try a ❺ _____ . That's just coffee topped with some steamed milk. You can also flavor it with vanilla ❻ _____ , or ❼ _____ .

Brenna: That could be tasty. I like the combination of coffee and milk.

Paul: Then I think you'll enjoy a ❽ _____ . That's half coffee and half steamed milk.

Brenna: Perfect. I'll have one of those.

Words to Remember

Choose the words in the box to complete the following sentences.

| decaffeinated | burst | latte | syrup |
| Americano | espresso | caramel | café au lait |

1. If you need some energy, drink a cup of _____ .
2. Marianne likes simple things, so she only drinks _____ coffee.
3. Wanting to add some flavor to his coffee, Mark decided to add some vanilla, or _____ .
4. I don't want to be up all night, so I'll just have a _____ coffee.
5. If you like coffee and milk together, try a latte or a _____ .

Get It Right

People often use the superlative form when they are describing food and drinks they really enjoy.

Example: I just went to the best coffee shop. The coffee they serve is the most delicious I've ever tasted. And the bread in their sandwich is the softest I've tried. It was incredible.

Your Turn: Write an e-mail to a friend describing a great experience you had eating at a coffee shop. Describe the food and drinks you tried using the superlative form to show how good it all was.

_____

_____

_____

_____

Grammar Bite

Superlatives are used when we want to show that something is greater than any other similar thing. When we use the superlative form, we use the following structure: **the + Adj. + est**

If the adjective is two or more syllables, use **most + Adj.**, and don't add the suffix *-est* to the adjective. But remember, there are some adjectives that don't follow the rule. For instance, the superlative form of *bad* is *worst*, and the superlative form of *good* is *best*. As for words that end in *y*, to change them to the superlative form we change the *y* to *i* and add *est*. If the adjective is two or more syllables, don't add *-est*; put *most* after *the*.

Examples:

- This is *the sweetest* cake I've ever had.
- This is *the most delicious* coffee.

- He is *the happiest* boy I've ever seen.
- Rex is *the friendliest* dog in the world.

Give It a Try

Use the following noun and adjective combinations to write sentences using the superlative form.

1. bitter, coffee, ever had
   This is the bitterest coffee I've ever had.
2. the shop, delicious, sandwich

   _____

3. my mom, tasty, donut

   _____

4. hot, soup, of all

   _____

5. I think, good, bagel

   _____

Prepare Yourself

Look at the pictures below of people eating and hanging out in a coffee shop.

writing

studying

chatting

reading

working

celebrating

Activity 1

With a partner, take turns answering the following questions about the pictures above.

1. What is your main reason for going to a coffee shop?
2. Do you think a coffee shop is a good place to get work done? Why or why not?
3. When you go to a coffee shop, what do you usually order?
4. Describe your favorite coffee shop. What is the atmosphere like? How are the staff?

Activity 2

Pretend you own a coffee shop and design a menu. Then, find a partner and have him / her place an order. You should be able to describe the foods and drinks on your menu. Then, change roles. Read you partner's menu and place an order.

Useful Expressions

- I want to get something *sweet / healthy*.
- I like *black coffee* because it is *bitter*.
- The *bagels* here are especially good.
- This shop's specialty is the *café mocha*, so I'll have to order one of those.

Listening

Track 31 You are going to hear Mark and Dianne talking about buying groceries. Listen and write down the items each person wants to buy.

Mark wants:

Dianne wants:

Vocabulary

Use the words from the box to complete the paragraph below.

| item | budget | exchange rate | cart | convert |

When you travel, one of the toughest things is saving money. After all, there are so many things to spend money on. One of the things that will eat up a lot of your ❶ _____ is food. But there are a few ways to save money on food while you're on the road. First of all, buy food at a supermarket whenever you can rather than eating out. But pay close attention to each ❷ _____ you buy. Don't fill up your ❸ _____ with junk. Buy only what you need, and look for things that are on sale. Also, keep an eye on the prices. Chances are they'll be in a foreign currency. So you must know the ❹ _____. Then you can ❺ _____ the prices to the currency in your home country before you buy. Is it really a good deal? Remember, save money, and travel longer.

Grammar

Fill in the blanks with the superlative form of the adjective in the parenthesis.

1. This is the _____ coffee I've ever tasted. (strong)

2. This is the _____ sandwich I've ever had. (bad)

3. Isn't this the _____ cake in the world? (good)

4. Be careful. This place serves the _____ soup I've ever tried. (hot)

5. My mother makes the _____ desserts. (tasty)

Reading

Fill in the blanks with the correct word. The first letters are given.

There are so many different kinds of coffee to choose from nowadays. If you walk into a coffee shop and just order a "coffee," the clerk will probably look at you with a confused look on his or her face. Whenever I go to my favorite coffee shop, I usually keep it simple. I order an Ame_____, which is just hot water and esp_____. That's the thing that gives you a quick burst of energy to keep you awake. If I don't need energy, I order a dec_____ coffee. That's coffee without the caffeine. Sometimes I'll have a la_____. That's just coffee topped with steamed milk. If I want a bit of flavor, I add va_____ syrup or car_____ to it. It's sweet, but a little sweetness now and then never hurt anybody. What do you get when you go for a cup of coffee?

Conversation

Complete Jacob's replies with the proper response from the box below.

> A. Those are too oily for me.
> B. Oh, I've had those before. They're nice and crunchy.
> C. Does it have to be hot food? I can't really handle it.

Terri: Let's get something spicy for lunch today. I know a great place at the market.

Jacob: _____

Terri: No problem. We can get something mild. What about dessert? I know a good place to get a deep fried donut.

Jacob: _____

Terri: What about a cookie then? My favorite bakery is at the market, too.

Jacob: _____

Terri: Great! Let's go.

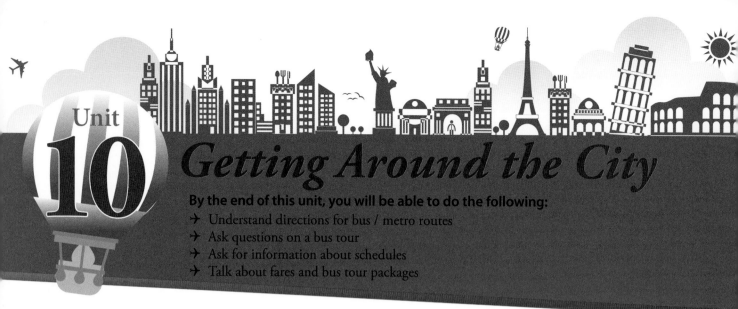

By the end of this unit, you will be able to do the following:

→ Understand directions for bus / metro routes
→ Ask questions on a bus tour
→ Ask for information about schedules
→ Talk about fares and bus tour packages

Before We Go

Look at the pictures of these common kinds of transportation that we encounter in a trip. Match the numbered items (1-6) with the correct term in the box.

| airplane | bus | ferry | subway | taxi | train |

❶

❷

❸

❹

❺

❻

Useful Expressions

- What do you see on the front of the *bus*?
- I can see the route number. It's *number 10*.
- What does the *bus stop* sign say?
- The *bus* is heading toward Potsdam Square.
- This is the earliest *train* to Paris.

Conversation 1

Track 32 Anna is at a bus stop in Barcelona, Spain, looking at the route map and trying to figure out which bus to take. A stranger, Pablo, notices her confusion. Listen to the conversation and fill in the missing words.

Pablo: Hello. Do you need some help?

Anna: Oh! Yeah, I'm having trouble figuring out the best ❶ _____.

Pablo: Well, the bus system can be a bit confusing here. There are a lot of ❷ _____.

Anna: My town only has four, and the ❸ _____ is pretty cheap.

Pablo: Barcelona's ❹ _____ is definitely bigger than that! So, where do you want to go?

Anna: I want to go to that big church, the Sagrada Família. I hear it's the most beautiful building in Barcelona.

Pablo: Well, it's certainly the most unique! The ❺ _____ is the fastest option. It will take about 30 minutes. Take the L7 line to Provença; that's the fourth stop. Then, ❻ _____ to the L5 line. You'll only have two stops before you reach Sagrada Família.

Anna: I know the metro might be faster than the bus, but I don't want to be underground. I would like to see some of the city as I travel.

Pablo: I understand. In that case, you can take bus number 58 from here.

Anna: Will that take me ❼ _____ there?

Pablo: No. After six stops, ❽ _____ and transfer to the number 34. Then, get off when you see the Sagrada Família. If you're going to take the bus a lot, get the one-day travel card. It's the cheapest option.

Words to Remember

Choose the words in the box to complete the sentences.

route	metro	bus line	transfer
straight	transit system	get off	fare

1. What is the quickest _____ from here to Main Street?

2. The _____ for the bus is $2.

3. We'll have to _____ to another train.

4. This is our stop. Let's _____ here.

5. Berlin is known for its clean and reliable _____.

 **Reading**

Track 33 Read this brochure about different travel card and ticket options for Barcelona's transit system.

Welcome to Barcelona, the most beautiful city in Spain!

We have so much for you to do and see all over the city, and you don't want to miss out on anything. With our fabulous public transportation system, you don't have to! To find out which is the right ticket for you, read the information below.

- **Single Journey Ticket:** This is the best ticket for people who have just one place to go. For only €2, you can get to nearly anywhere in the city.

- **One-Day Travel Card (T-Dia):** If you will be taking more than three trips in a single day, this ticket is the easiest and the cheapest option. It lets you travel as much as you want in a single day. One zone costs €7.25, but the greatest deal is to buy one for all six zones at a price of €20.65.

- **T-10 Card:** This card is the smartest choice for people who will travel a few times a day but will be in Barcelona for several days. It covers ten trips. Prices start as low as €9.80 for one zone.

- **T-50/30 vs. Monthly Travel Card (T-Mes):** The most enjoyable trips are the ones that last longer. If you are going to be in Barcelona for a month, you have two choices. The T-50/30 allows 50 trips within 30 days. The T-Mes has no limit on the number of trips within 30 days. For those on a budget, the T-50/30 may be the most reasonable choice. If you plan on more than two trips a day, though, the T-Mes is the wisest choice.

Give It a Try

Based on the article, choose the correct answer for the following questions.

1. Who should buy a single journey ticket?
   a. Someone taking multiple trips.
   b. Someone staying in the city for a month.
   c. Someone traveling for an entire day.
   d. Someone who only has one place to go.

2. Who would be best served by buying a monthly travel card?
   a. Someone staying at least 30 days.
   b. Someone who only has one place to go.
   c. Someone living in the city permanently.
   d. Someone spending the day in the city.

3. What is the main purpose of this passage?
   a. To tell you where to stay in the city
   b. To show which ticket or card is best for you
   c. To tell tourists how to be safe in Barcelona
   d. To talk about the history of Barcelona

4. When do you get the best deal with the T-Dia Card?
   a. When you buy a card for two zones.
   b. When you buy a card for less than five zones.
   c. When you buy a card for all six zones.
   d. When you buy a card for just one zone.

5. When should you buy a T-10 card?
   a. When you need to stay in the city for one month.
   b. When you need to take a few trips over several days.
   c. When you need to take three trips in a single day.
   d. When you need to take one trip a single time.

Conversation 2

 Track 34 Anna has decided to take a bus tour of Barcelona. As she rides through the city, she talks to the tour guide about the sights of the city. Listen to the conversation and fill in the missing words.

Tour guide: Barcelona is a city filled with history. So many interesting things happened here.

Anna: Oh! That's pretty! What is that?

Tour guide: That's the Royal ❶ _____. It was built in the 1800s, and its ❷ _____ and restaurants are visited by many ❸ _____ and tourists. See those lanterns? They were designed by Antoni Gaudí.

Anna: Who's that?

Tour guide: He's a famous Spanish ❹ _____. We will have time later for a closer look at other places that were ❺ _____ and built by Gaudí.

Anna: Actually, I was shown a park earlier that has Gaudí's art in it.

Tour guide: Park Güell? Gaudí worked on it for 14 years before it was finished.

Anna: I was really ❻ _____ by the ❼ _____ lizard ❽ _____ at the entrance. Wasn't that also made by Gaudí?

Tour guide: That's right. It has been left to guard the park for nearly 100 years.

Anna: Are we also going by the ❾ _____ that was created by Gaudí?

Tour guide: Actually, that church was started by someone else, and then the project was taken over by Gaudí. But only a quarter of it was done by the time he died. The work has been continued by many other people since.

Anna: I can't wait to see it!

Words to Remember

Choose the words in the box to complete the following sentences.

plaza	nightclub	local	architect
impress	mosaic	statue	basilica	design

1. If you like to design things, you should be a(n) _____.
2. Mostly _____ come to this restaurant; very few tourists.
3. Michelangelo's *David* is one of the world's most famous _____.
4. Carlos was _____ by the tour guide's knowledge of the city.
5. Lots of people came to the _____ to dance and have fun.

71

 # Get It Right

Tour guides often use the passive voice when they are describing an attraction on a tour.

Example: To your left, you can see the Hospital of Saint Paul. The current building was built in the twentieth century, but the first Hospital of Saint Paul was founded in the 1400s. It is located in the center of Barcelona. It was designed by Guillem d'Abriell, and the first stone was put into place in 1401. Most of the work was finished by 1414. In the sixteenth century, much of the building was changed. By the end of the 1800s, it was thought to be too small to serve as the main hospital, so this new building was opened.

Your Turn: Imagine you are a tour guide in Barcelona and are describing Casa Batlló to a group of tourists. Search useful information to write your speech, and use the passive voice as much as possible.

_____

_____

_____

_____

 # Grammar Bite

The passive voice can be used to put emphasis on the object of a sentence or if the subject (the person or thing doing the action) is unknown.

To form the passive voice, use the correct form of *be* and the past participle of the verb.

Normal: Gaudí designed the lanterns.

Passive: The lanterns were designed by Gaudí.

Note: If the person or thing that caused the action is included, put *by* in front of it.

 # Give It a Try

Change each of the following sentences into the passive voice.

1. The tour guide tells a story.

_____

2. People built the house in 1893.

_____

3. The maid cleans the hotel room.

_____

4. Anna visited Park Güell yesterday.

_____

5. Someone will open a new nightclub in the plaza.

_____

Prepare Yourself

Look at the transit map below. On the map, you will see popular tourist attractions, routes, and stops for different kinds of transportation: metro (subway), bus, tram, and ferry.

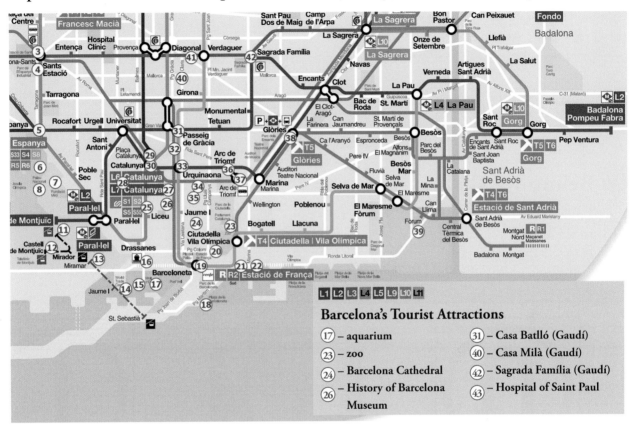

Barcelona's Tourist Attractions

- (17) – aquarium
- (23) – zoo
- (24) – Barcelona Cathedral
- (26) – History of Barcelona Museum
- (31) – Casa Batlló (Gaudí)
- (40) – Casa Milà (Gaudí)
- (42) – Sagrada Família (Gaudí)
- (43) – Hospital of Saint Paul

Activity 1

With a partner, take turns asking and answering the following questions about the transit map above.

1. In which area of the city can you find the tram?
2. What station has the most metro lines connecting to it?
3. How can you get from the Barcelona Cathedral to the Sagrada Família?
4. Which metro lines run closest to the water?

Activity 2

Plan your own tour of Barcelona using the public transportation system. Make notes about your tour route below and what you will see. Then, share your plans with a partner.

Useful Expressions

- I will begin my tour at *Park Güell*.
- From there, I will take *the bus* to *Casa Mila*.
- I will get out at *Girona* station and *walk to the next sight*.
- I will end my day at *Sagrada Família*.

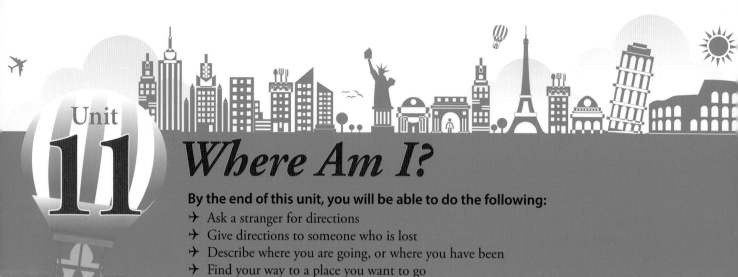

Unit 11

Where Am I?

By the end of this unit, you will be able to do the following:

➜ Ask a stranger for directions
➜ Give directions to someone who is lost
➜ Describe where you are going, or where you have been
➜ Find your way to a place you want to go

Before We Go

Look at the following pictures of direction signs. Match the pictures (1-5) with the correct term in the box.

| stop | turn around / turn back | go straight | turn right | turn left |

❶ _____   ❷ _____   ❸ _____

❹ _____   ❺ _____

Useful Expressions

- Excuse me, can you tell me how to get to the *Natural History Museum*?
- Go straight for *two blocks* and then *turn right*.
- I was wondering if you could tell me how to get to the *library*.
- Pardon me, I seem to be lost.

 Conversation 1

 Track 35 Stephanie is walking around in a new city, but she is lost. She meets Dan, a local, and decides to ask him for directions. Listen to the conversation and fill in the missing words.

Stephanie: Excuse me, I seem to be ❶ _____. I was wondering if you could point me in the right ❷ _____.

Dan: I can certainly try. Where do you want to go?

Stephanie: I'm ❸ _____ the St. James Cathedral. I thought it is on this street, but I can't seem to find it.

Dan: Oh, I know where that is. It's on 2nd Avenue, near the ❹ _____ with Rogers Road. You're on the right street, just at the wrong intersection.

Stephanie: OK, which way should I go.

Dan: Just go straight that way, then ❺ _____ the street. You can't miss it.

Stephanie: Great, thanks very much. Oh, one more thing, if you don't mind. I was also planning to visit the Waterton Aquarium this afternoon. Is that ❻ _____ here?

Dan: Actually it's a bit ❼ _____. You could walk there, but it will take about 30 minutes.

Stephanie: I don't mind walking. Where should I go?

Dan: From the church, head east for four ❽ _____, then north for two. From there you should see signs pointing the way.

Stephanie: Perfect. I should be able to find it without any trouble. Thanks again.

Dan: It's my pleasure.

Words to Remember

Choose the words in the box to complete the sentences.

intersection	near	look for	block
direction	cross	lost	far away

1. Marcus checked the map to see if he was going in the right _____.

2. To get there, just go straight for two _____.

3. The bank is _____ here. It's just two minutes away on foot.

4. That store is on the other side of the street. You'll have to _____.

5. Pardon me, I'm _____ the nearest restaurant.

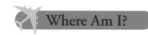

 Reading

Track 36 Read this article about asking for directions.

If you're lost, the quickest way to get where you want to go is to ask someone for directions. It doesn't take a rocket scientist to figure that out. But did you know that asking for directions when you're lost can help you save money, and help the environment? It's true. A recent study undertaken by a British insurer called Shielas' Wheels found that women are far more likely to ask for directions than men are. This probably isn't news to most people, but the rest of the study's findings likely are. Because men are less likely to ask for directions, they spend an extra US$3,000 on average during the course of their lifetime. This is due to the fact that they will have to travel greater distances to get where they need to go. In fact, men, on average, have to travel an extra 276 miles per year due to the fact that they're too stubborn to just ask someone where a place is. This means men have to buy more fuel, which in turn harms the environment.

The study also found that two in five men will tell a passenger in their vehicle they know where they are going, when in fact they have no idea where they are going. Meanwhile, 75 percent of women have no problem pulling over and asking a stranger for directions. All drivers, male and female, prefer to ask a woman for directions rather than a man, according to the study.

Give It a Try

A. Based on the article, circle True or False for the following sentences.

1. Asking for directions is bad for the environment.   True / False
2. Asking for directions can cost you money.   True / False
3. Men are less likely than women to ask for directions.   True / False
4. Men will likely spend less money than women during their lifetime.   True / False
5. Women and men prefer to ask a woman for directions.   True / False

B. Based on the article, choose the correct answer for the following questions.

1. What is the main topic of this passage?
   a. The best ways to save money.
   b. Reasons why asking for directions is a good idea.
   c. Who has a better sense of direction.
   d. A few ways to help the environment.

2. What is true of forty percent of men, according to the study mentioned in the article?
   a. They would rather ask a man for directions.
   b. They will drive an extra 276 miles.
   c. They will lie about knowing where they are going.
   d. They would rather be driven by a woman.

3. What is true of three-quarters of women, according to the study?
   a. They have never asked for directions.
   b. They don't mind asking for directions.
   c. They are confident giving directions.
   d. They refuse to ask for directions.

Conversation 2

Track 37 Mike has now spent a few days in a new city, and is confident about giving others directions. Another traveler, Christine, stops to ask him about how to get somewhere. Listen to the conversation and fill in the missing words.

Christine: Excuse me, but do you live here?

Mike: No, I'm just a tourist, but I've been here for a while. I know my way around pretty well. How can I help you?

Christine: Do you know ❶ _____ it is to the coliseum from here?

Mike: It's quite far away, but it's within walking ❷ _____. You just ❸ _____ this road until it ends, turn right, walk straight for three blocks, then turn left.

Christine: How long do you think it will take to walk there?

Mike: ❹ _____ 45 minutes, I'd say.

Christine: OK, and you say I should just ❺ _____ down this road until it ends, right?

Mike: Exactly. Or, you can take a ❻ _____ through City Park. That will save you about 10 minutes.

Christine: How do I get to the park?

Mike: Just head down this road until you walk ❼ _____ an ice cream shop. You'll see the park on your right.

Christine: Great. I just hope I don't end up going the ❽ _____ again.

Mike: I'm sure you'll be all right. Good luck!

Words to Remember

Choose the words in the box to complete the following sentences.

shortcut	how far	wrong way	past
continue	distance	follow	about

1. I'm not exactly sure how long it will take to get there, but I think _____ ten minutes.

2. You don't need to make any turns. Just _____ this road.

3. _____ down this street, and you'll see the museum.

4. Travis went _____ the deli and found the market.

5. Bryce has lived here all his life, so he knows the _____ to the lake.

Get It Right

People have to use prepositions of place and prepositional phrases when giving directions.

Example: Turn left at the next intersection. You'll find the clothing shop next to the diner.

Your Turn: Write an e-mail to a friend describing the best way to get between various places in your hometown that you feel are worth visiting for travelers. Use as many prepositions of time and place and prepositional phrases as you can.

_____

_____

_____

_____

Grammar Bite

We use prepositions of place to describe where something is. Common prepositions of place include *in, on, under, over / above, next to, between, near, in front of, behind*.

Examples:

* The music shop is *next to* the restaurant.
* The restaurant is *behind* the convenience store.
* The furniture store is *above* the bowling alley.

When using prepositional phrases, it's important to remember to not leave out part of the phrase.

Examples:

* Can I sit next you? ☒
* Can I sit next *to* you. ☑

Give It a Try

Use the prepositions in the box to complete the sentences.

on	next	above	beneath

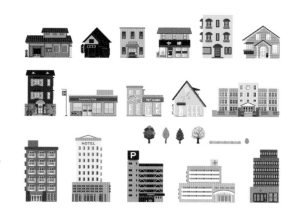

1. Put the book _____ the shelf.
2. There is a bookstore _____ to the café.
3. The mountain rises _____ the clouds.
4. A bird landed _____ the branch.
5. A whale was swimming _____ the waves.

Prepare Yourself

Take a look at this picture of a woman and man arguing over the correct directions.

Activity 1

With a partner, take turns answering the following questions about the picture above.

1. Are you comfortable asking another person for directions? Why or why not?

2. If someone asks you for directions, but you don't know the way, what would you do?

3. Have you ever gotten lost? If so, what did you do?

4. These days, you can use services like Google Maps to get directions instantly. Do you think getting lost is a thing of the past? Why or why not?

Activity 2

Here is a map of the Paris city center. Pick a starting point, any place on the map, and take notes about where you would like to go in the city. Then, describe where you would go to a partner, giving as many details as possible about directions. Then, have your partner describe where they would go to you.

Useful Expressions

- I would start my day at the *Eiffel tower*.
- From there, I would walk *two blocks east* to the *Louvre Museum*.
- After that, I would head *south* toward *the Arc de Triomphe*.
- Finally, I would walk *three blocks left, turn right*, and end my day at *the Grand Palais*.

Unit 12

I'm Sick.

By the end of this unit, you will be able to do the following:

→ Describe your symptoms to a doctor
→ Discuss how often/when to take medication
→ Talk about minor health problems
→ Understand medical advice

Before We Go

Look at these pictures of a few symptoms of common illnesses. Match the pictures (1-6) to the proper terms in the box.

| stomachache | earache | headache | sore throat | runny nose | coughing / sneezing |

❶

❷

❸

❹

❺

❻

Useful Expressions

- I haven't been feeling well the past couple of *days*.
- My *throat* is *sore*.
- I'm *coughing* all the time.
- I have a *pounding headache*.

Conversation 1

Track 38 Jessica is traveling overseas, and has suddenly become ill. She is now at the clinic, talking to a doctor. Listen to the conversation and fill in the missing words.

Doctor: What seems to be the matter today, miss?

Jessica: I think I have a ❶ _____, doctor. I've been running hot and cold since last night.

Doctor: OK, let's just take your ❷ _____ first. Just put this ❸ _____ under your tongue and hold it there until I say.

Jessica: OK.

Doctor: Ah, yes. You're burning up. Are you experiencing any other ❹ _____?

Jessica: Yes, I've been feeling sick to my stomach as well.

Doctor: All right. I'm just going to check your ❺ _____ and your ❻ _____. These are just routine tests to determine exactly what is wrong.

Jessica: No problem, I've been through this before.

Doctor: When was the last time you had a full ❼ _____?

Jessica: Just over a year ago. I try to go for one every year, but I've been traveling a lot this year.

Doctor: I understand. It's likely nothing serious, but I'd like to do a ❽ _____ just to be safe. Are you afraid of needles?

Jessica: No, doctor, I've had blood taken before. It doesn't bother me.

Words to Remember

Choose the words in the box to complete the sentences.

pulse	*fever*	*blood pressure*	*temperature*
thermometer	*discomfort*	*blood test*	*physical examination*

1. The _____ read 37 degrees Celsius.

2. Your forehead feels hot. Perhaps you have a _____.

3. It's a good idea to get a full _____ once per year.

4. "Are you experiencing any _____, such as stomach pain?" asked the doctor.

5. The doctor checked my _____, and found that my heart rate was normal.

I'm Sick.

 Reading

Track 39 Read this article about taking care of your health while traveling.

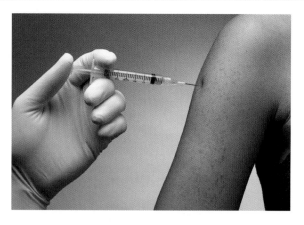

Before you hit the road, you should take some time to think about your health. What would you do if you became ill while traveling? Can you afford to pay large medical bills if something bad happens while you're abroad? Hopefully it never comes to this, but there are a few things every traveler should do before they set out on their journey. First of all, get immunized. There are many resources online which tell you which diseases you need to get immunized against depending on the country or countries you'll be visiting. Go to your local clinic and get the shots. Yes, your chances of getting something like malaria may be small, but it's always better to be safe than sorry.

Secondly, get some type of travel health insurance. It's usually not that expensive, and if you do get sick or injured while abroad, it can save you a lot of money. Hospital bills can add up quickly, depending on where you are traveling. Health insurance can mean the difference between continuing your trip once you're well again, and having to go home. Lastly, get the address and phone number for your home country's consulate in each of the countries you'll be visiting. In the case of a medical emergency, they may be able to assist you in some way. It also helps to familiarize yourself with the local hospital conditions in the countries you'll travel to before you leave on your trip. Keep these tips in mind, and stay healthy!

Give It a Try

A. Based on the article, circle True or False for the following sentences.

1. Hospital bills are usually cheaper in foreign countries.   True / False
2. Getting health insurance is a good idea when traveling.   True / False
3. Consulates can't help you if you have a health emergency abroad.   True / False
4. You should get the proper shots before you travel.   True / False
5. Know the hospital conditions in the countries you'll visit beforehand. True / False

B. Based on the article, choose the correct answer for the following questions.

1. What is the main purpose of this article?
   a. To show that hospital bills add up quickly
   b. To prove that getting treatment overseas is safe
   c. To give tips about travel and your health
   d. To explain why travel insurance is unnecessary

2. Why is it useful to get the information for your home country's consulate?
   a. They can help if you have medical problems.
   b. They can treat you for free.
   c. They can provide you with health insurance.
   d. They can send a doctor to your hotel or hostel.

Conversation 2

Track 40 Jessica has now finished her doctor's appointment and is at the pharmacy. She is discussing her medication with the pharmacist. Listen to the conversation and fill in the missing words.

Pharmacist: Take a moment to read through your ❶ _____ and see if you have any questions.

Jessica: Which ❷ _____ is for my stomach?

Pharmacist: Those ❸ _____ are in this bag here.

Jessica: And ❹ _____ am I to take those?

Pharmacist: Take one pill three times ❺ _____ after meals.

Jessica: OK, that seems easy enough. Are there any side effects for any of these medications?

Pharmacist: You may experience some ❻ _____, but that's all.

Jessica: Anything else I should know?

Pharmacist: Just remember not to ❼ _____ these medications with any others. Do you currently have any other prescriptions?

Jessica: No, just this one.

Pharmacist: Then there shouldn't be any ❽ _____. If you have any questions at all, feel free to give us a call.

Jessica: Thanks for your help.

Words to Remember

Choose the words in the box to complete the following sentences.

per day	pill	prescription	how often
combine	medication	drowsiness	complications

1. Helen felt sleepy because the medicine caused _____.

2. Remember to take one of these _____ every morning until they're gone.

3. Jerome has to take several different _____ to cure his illness.

4. This medicine should be taken three times _____.

5. _____ should I take this medicine?

 Get It Right

We often use the Present Continuous form to describe our symptoms to a doctor.

Example:

I am not feeling very well. I am experiencing a sore throat, and I am always coughing.

Your Turn: Pretend you are sending a text message to a friend who is a doctor. You are asking your friend for medical advice. Describe your symptoms using the Present Continuous form.

Grammar Bite

We use the Present Continuous form to talk about things that are happening now. To express things in the Present Continuous form, we must use *-ing* verbs. Remember, if the verb ends in *e*, delete the *e* before adding *-ing*.

Examples:

- I am not *feeling* well.
- He is *feeling* sick.

- She is *doing* well.
- Things are *moving* quickly.

Give It a Try

Take the following combinations of words and use them to write sentences in the Present Continuous form.

1. She, cough

_____

2. He, sore throat

_____

3. Jane, runny nose

_____

4. Todd, see the doctor

_____

5. Brent, go to the clinic

_____

Prepare Yourself

Look at the pictures of various patients sitting in a hospital waiting room with different injuries or medical problems.

back pain

neck pain

arm fracture

sprained ankle

allergy

 Activity 1

With a partner, take turns answering the following questions about the pictures above.

1. What are the best ways to make sure you stay healthy while abroad?

2. What would you do if you were facing a large hospital bill while traveling?

3. Would you rather be treated for an illness abroad, or cut your trip short and return home for treatment? Explain your answer.

4. What is the worst part about going to the hospital / clinic for you and why?

Activity 2

Imagine that you are feeling ill and have to go see a doctor. Take notes on the various things you would have to do at the clinic. For example, first you would have to check in with a nurse at the reception desk. Describe all the things you would have to do to a partner, and then have your partner do the same.

Useful Expressions

- First, I would *check in* at the *reception desk*.
- Next, I would *have a seat* in the *waiting room*.
- Eventually, a nurse would *call my number*.
- After seeing the doctor, I would *pick up my prescription*.

Listening

Track 41 You are going to hear a conversation. Are the statements below true or false?

1. Tammy asks Fred for assistance.   True / False

2. Tammy wants to go to the central part of the city.   True / False

3. Fred doesn't need to see the route map.   True / False

4. Tammy wants to go to a sporting event.   True / False

5. Tammy can't take a bus directly to his destination.   True / False

6. Fred says Tammy will have to wait a long time for the bus.   True / False

Vocabulary

Complete the passage with the words in the box.

impress	local	architect	design

Whenever I travel to a new city, I'm very interested in checking out the interesting buildings. That's

probably because I want to become a(n) ❶ _____ . I've always been interested in

the unique ❷ _____ of certain buildings. If I don't know what I should go see, I

ask a(n) ❸ _____ . They always know best. That reminds me of the time I was in

Bilbao, Spain. I asked someone from the city what I should see, and he recommended the Guggenheim

Museum. I was so ❹ _____ by the creativity Frank Gehry used when designing it. It

inspired me to work even harder to achieve my dream.

Grammar

Choose the correct preposition for each sentence.

1. Hang your coat up *(on / in)* the closet.

2. Bobby dropped his laundry *(on / in)* the floor.

3. The playground is next *(to / on)* top of the school.

4. Dave lives on the second floor, *(above / under)* a convenience store on the first floor.

5. The library is *(between / in front of)* two clothing shops, one on either side.

Reading

Complete the words or phrases in the passage. The first letters are given.

I live in New York, and we get a lot of tourists here. They often ask me for directions. Luckily, I know

my way ar ▓▓▓▓▓▓ pretty well. The other day, a man walked up to me and asked if I

knew the way to Madison Square Garden. I told him to fo ▓▓▓▓▓▓ Fifth Avenue for

ab ▓▓▓▓▓▓ three blocks. Then, I told him to ta ▓▓▓▓▓▓ the subway to

Broadway. Then, he could con ▓▓▓▓▓▓ walking south for just a few more blocks, and

he'd be there. He was so happy for the good directions that he shook my hand. I really like helping people

discover my city.

Conversation

Choose the correct lines from the box to complete the conversation.

> A. No problem. I've been through this before.
> B. They don't bother me at all.
> C. I have a sore throat, and I'm coughing all the time.
> D. Yes, my stomach also doesn't feel well.
> E. About two years ago, I think.

Ken: What seems to be the matter today?

Erica: ▓▓▓

Ken: Are you experiencing any other symptoms?

Erica: ▓▓▓

Ken: OK, I think we're going to have to run a few tests. Just routine things such as a blood pressure check, and we'll take your temperature.

Erica: ▓▓▓

Ken: When was the last time you had a physical examination?

Erica: ▓▓▓

Ken: I see. It's probably nothing serious, but I'd like to do a blood test, just to be safe. Are you afraid of needles?

Erica: ▓▓▓

Ken: OK then, let's get started.

Unit 13

Museums for Free

By the end of this unit, you will be able to do the following:

→ Ask where to find different exhibits or places in a museum
→ Talk about history and artifacts from the past
→ Find out what is showing at a museum
→ Have a conversation based on what you learn at a museum

 Before We Go

Look at the following pictures of things you would commonly find in a museum. Match the pictures (1-6) with the proper terms in the box.

| artifacts | guide | sculpture | ticket booth | display | souvenirs |

❶

❷

❸

❹

❺

❻

Useful Expressions

- This *display* comes from the *Cambrian period*.
- What are these interesting *artifacts*?
- Do you know how old this *statue* is?
- When was this *settlement* discovered?

 Conversation 1

Track 42 Ryan and Sarah are going to the Natural History Museum. They walk up to the ticket booth to speak to a member of the museum's staff, Vivian. Listen to the conversation and fill in the missing words.

Ryan: Hi there, we'd like two ❶ _____ please. How much are they?

Vivian: Actually, there's no charge for tickets to see the Natural History Museum. Though we do take ❷ _____. But that's entirely up to you.

Sarah: Free? That's perfect. It's such a big museum. I doubt we can see it all in one day. What do you recommend seeing?

Vivian: I'd recommend checking out the Dino Days ❸ _____. It's only here for a few more days, and then it will be shipped off to another museum. There are some extremely rare specimens ❹ _____.

Ryan: I'll definitely check that out. What else?

Vivian: We also have ❺ _____ and ❻ _____ available. They're both a great way to get some extra information, and also free of charge.

Sarah: Let's take a guided tour. That way I can ask questions if I have any.

Ryan: I'm sure you'll have a lot.

Vivian: That's perfectly all right. Our ❼ _____ are happy to answer any questions you might have.

Sarah: Oh, I have one already. Do you have a ❽ _____? I want to pick something up for my cousins.

Vivian: Certainly, it's just to the left of the main entrance.

Ryan: But let's hit the gift shop on the way out. Dino Days, here we come!

Words to Remember

Choose the words in the box to complete the sentences.

guided tour	donation	gift shop	tickets
audio tour	exhibition	on display	volunteer

1. Stan bought two _____ and went into the movie theater.

2. There are many sculptures that are _____ in the museum.

3. Vera doesn't get paid for her work. She's a _____.

4. If you want to buy a souvenir, then go to the _____.

5. There is a(n) _____ of some of Van Gogh's paintings at the museum today.

 Reading

Track 43 **Read this article about Museum of Tolerance in Los Angeles, USA.**

There are museums dedicated to history, and museums dedicated to art. There's even a museum dedicated to torture in London. But there's one special museum in Los Angeles that has an entirely different theme. It's called the Museum of Tolerance. It's a museum that strives to help people confront things like racism and prejudice, largely through the lens of the Holocaust. The Museum of Tolerance first opened its doors to the public in 1993. Since then, it has won wide acclaim from world leaders and international organizations. There are interactive exhibits to take in, two theaters, a research floor, and a gallery for special exhibitions. And it's not hard to experience the whole thing in a day. Tours of the place are self-guided, and take about two-and-a-half hours, on average.

The museum's reputation has grown to the point where it is one of the must-see attractions of L.A. About a quarter of a million visitors stream through its doors every year. It's a good place to go to learn about the nature of mankind, and think about how we can avoid such large scale tragedies in the future, all while learning about an important part of our history. If you find yourself in L.A., stop by the Museum of Tolerance for a life-changing experience.

Give It a Try

A. Based on the article, circle True or False for the following sentences.

1. The museum of tolerance is dedicated to events after 1993.   True / False
2. There are no interactive exhibits at the MOT.   True / False
3. The MOT can be seen in a single day.   True / False
4. Tours of the MOT take about 2.5 days.   True / False
5. Almost a million people see the MOT each year.   True / False

B. Based on the article, choose the correct answer for the following questions.

1. What is the main purpose of this article?
   a. To mention things to do in L.A.
   b. To examine events that happened in 1993
   c. To portray a unique museum
   d. To discuss the importance of a historical event

2. Based on the information in the passage, what can we assume the author's opinion of the museum is?
   a. Indifferent   **b.** Critical   **c.** Negative   **d.** Favorable

3. What can the MOT help us do, according to the article?
   a. Help us avoid big catastrophes in the future
   b. Help us forget about terrible things in the past
   c. Help us win acclaim from world leaders
   d. Help us learn about the history of Los Angeles

Conversation 2

Track 44 Ryan and Sarah are now touring through the museum with their guide, Xavier. Listen to the conversation and fill in the missing words.

Xavier: And if you'll direct your attention to this display ❶ _____, you'll see a vase dating back to the 17th ❷ _____.

Ryan: Wow, it's in such good ❸ _____.

Sarah: Yes, it's very ❹ _____. Why is it so free of damage?

Xavier: It was actually stored with a private ❺ _____ for many decades. A very wealthy family owned it, and then donated it to our museum.

Sarah: I like the artwork on it. Does it mean anything?

Xavier: ❻ _____ believe the decorations on this vase and others of its kind told the story of an ❼ _____ ruling family. You can see some of the family symbols hidden within the artwork.

Sarah: Oh, yeah, I can see it. And what's that over there?

Xavier: Here we have a set of tools from the Stone ❽ _____. These were excavated from a ❾ _____ not far from here, in what used to be an ancient settlement.

Ryan: What was that one used for?

Xavier: That was used for cutting wood. And the one beside it was used for cooking.

Ryan: It's hard to believe how far we've come since then.

Xavier: Indeed. Now if you'll follow me this way, we have much more to see.

Words to Remember

Choose the words in the box to complete the following sentences.

case	age	site	collection	well-preserved
century	historian	ancient	condition	

1. This car is in excellent _____.
2. Karen has a lot of CDs in her _____.
3. All of these statues come from the Bronze _____.
4. This sculpture isn't just old, it's _____.
5. It's an old lamp, but it looks new because it has been _____.

Get It Right

We often use the Zero Conditional structure when making plans.

Example:

If we have enough time, we should check out the museum's main exhibition hall.

Pretend you are writing an e-mail to a friend, discussing your plan to visit a famous museum the following day. Use the Zero Conditional structure to tell your friend what you should see and do at the museum.

_____

_____

_____

Grammar Bite

The Zero Conditional structure is used to talk about something that is always true. In other words, it always happens as a result of something else that happens.

Examples:

- *If* I have time, I *will* go to the museum tomorrow.
- *If* I have extra money, I'*ll* take a long vacation.

You can also form the Zero Conditional structure using the Imperative form.

Example:

- *If* the smoke alarm goes off, everyone *must* exit the museum.
- *When* the school bell rings, everyone *must* go to class.

Or, you can form the Zero Conditional using a modal verb.

Example:

- *If* you show your passport, you *can* get into the museum for free.
- *If* you have a coupon, you *can* get a discount.

Give It a Try

From the following combinations, write out statements in the Zero Conditional form.

1. it will rain tomorrow / go to the park

_____

2. finish the museum tour before six / meet my parents for dinner

_____

3. go to Brad's house / he cooks for us

_____

4. people don't get enough sleep / they feel bad

_____

Prepare Yourself

Look at the pictures of various things you would see in a museum.

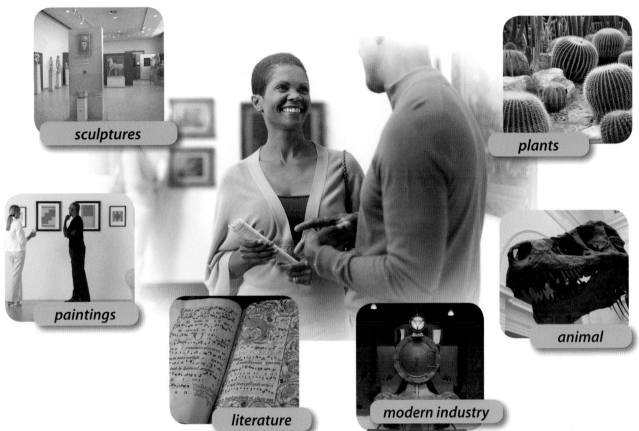

sculptures

plants

paintings

literature

modern industry

animal

Activity 1

With a partner, take turns answering the following questions about the pictures above.

1. When you are traveling, do you like going to museums? Why or why not?

2. What kind of museums do you prefer to visit? (art, natural history, other)

3. What can be gained from going to a museum?

4. Is a museum a good place to learn about local culture? Why or why not?

Activity 2

Look at the pictures above of various exhibits again. Take notes on which exhibits you would like to visit, and why you want to visit them. Further, try to suggest other kinds of exhibits you might like to see. Then, describe those exhibits to a partner, and talk about why you want to see them.

Useful Expressions

- The *Vikings exhibition* is a must-see, as *the Vikings are part of my family heritage*.
- I've always been interested in *money*, so I have to wander through *the ancient coins exhibit*.
- *Egypt* has fascinated me for a long time, so I have to check out the artifacts taken from *King Tut's tomb*.
- The exhibition on *medieval Japan* should be interesting. I'm intrigued by *Japanese culture*.

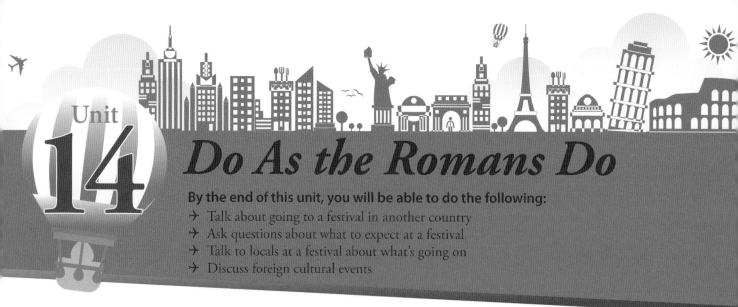

Do As the Romans Do

By the end of this unit, you will be able to do the following:

→ Talk about going to a festival in another country
→ Ask questions about what to expect at a festival
→ Talk to locals at a festival about what's going on
→ Discuss foreign cultural events

Before We Go

Look at the following pictures of things you would commonly find at a local cultural festival. Match the pictures (1-6) with the proper terms in the box.

food stand	*stage*	*costume*	*parade*	*flag*	*band*

① _____ ② _____ ③ _____

④ _____ ⑤ _____ ⑥ _____

Useful Expressions

- What time will the *performance* begin?
- What is the cultural significance of this *display*?

- How did *the festival* get started?
- Can you help me understand *what's going on here*?

Conversation 1

Track 45 Robert is in Munich for Oktoberfest. His local friend, Sasha, is showing him around and explaining the festivities to him. Listen to the conversation and fill in the missing words.

Robert: I can't believe I finally get to see this great ❶ _____. There's so much going on, I don't even know where to start.

Sasha: Well, first of all, it's not just about the party. There are a lot of ❷ _____ things to do.

Robert: Oh, yeah? Like what?

Sasha: For starters, there are the ❸ _____ German dance performances to take in.

Robert: I've never seen that before. Put that on our list.

Sasha: Another thing is all around you, the clothing. Do you see what that man over there is wearing? Those are called *lederhosen*. In the ❹ _____, German men would wear them when they had to do hard, physical work.

Robert: I was wondering what that was all about. And what's this music I'm hearing? It sounds so lively!

Sasha: That's traditional German ❺ _____ music. The ❻ _____ and tourists alike really get into it.

Robert: You'll have to teach me the words to some of the songs. But what about the best part? The food!

Sasha: Don't worry, we'll get to that. There are a lot of German ❼ _____ and snacks we can try.

Robert: I want to try a pretzel, and some pork knuckle, and...

Sasha: Whoa, slow down. We don't have to ❽ _____ everything ❾ _____ on one day. Let's pace ourselves.

Words to Remember

Choose the words in the box to complete the sentences.

traditional	past	folk	dish
festival	cultural	local	take in

1. Let's do something _____, like go to an art museum.

2. That happened in the _____—a very long time ago.

3. Did your father ever pass on any _____ stories to you?

4. Pad Thai is a _____ food Thai people have eaten for a long time.

5. There were so many _____ sitting on the table for us to try.

95

 # Reading

Track 46 **Read this article about some tips for attending Carnival in Brazil.**

If there is one festival in the world that you should definitely make time for, it's Brazilian Carnival. It's a huge celebration held every year from Friday to Tuesday before Ash Wednesday. As Wednesday marks the beginning of Lent, a 40-day period of fasting during which Catholics deprive themselves of at least one thing they enjoy to show their faith. So, before this tough period begins, people in Brazil throw a really, really big party. It sounds like a lot of fun, and it is, but there are a few things to keep in mind if you go.

First of all, wear clothing that you don't mind getting dirty. Carnival is hot, crowded, sweaty, and trucks routinely douse the crowd with water. In other words, wearing your best dress or shirt is probably not a good idea. Always plan for rain, too. It often showers during the day while Carnival is on. But umbrellas block everyone's view of the colorful floats going by and the celebration in general. Bring a light raincoat instead, just in case. And if you have valuables, such as a cell phone, put them in a plastic bag so they won't get ruined. As for your money, do as the locals do and put it in a money belt. Pickpockets are common, and they go for peoples' wallets. With that being said, Carnival is generally a safe event. Just keep your wits about you and, above all, have a fantastic time!

 # Give It a Try

A. Based on the article, circle True or False for the following sentences.

1.	It never rains during Carnival.	True / False
2.	Always wear your best clothing to Carnival.	True / False
3.	Bring a raincoat instead of an umbrella.	True / False
4.	Keep your cash in your wallet.	True / False
5.	Carnival is generally safe.	True / False

B. Based on the article, choose the correct answer for the following questions.

1. What happens after Carnival?
   a. Everyone in Brazil prepares for the rainy season.
   b. People give up things they enjoy for a while.
   c. Lots of colorful floats go by.
   d. Another big party takes place.

2. What do we know about pickpockets?
   a. They appear at Carnival once in a while.　　**c.** They leave people at Carnival alone.
   b. They are common at Carnival.　　**d.** They can't be found at Carnival.

3. What is the writer's overall opinion of Carnival?
   a. It's safe and you should go.　　**c.** It's expensive and only for rich people.
   b. It's dangerous and should be avoided.　　**d.** It's overrated and not worth checking out.

Conversation 2

Track 47 Robert and Sasha are still at Oktoberfest. Sasha is letting him know some dos and don'ts for the festival. Listen to the conversation and fill in the missing words.

Robert: I'm having so much fun so far.

Sasha: That's great. It looks like the party is in full swing now.

Robert: But I still feel like I ❶ _____ like a sore thumb. I want to ❷ _____ !

Sasha: Well, take a look around. What do you see?

Robert: Everyone is dancing to the music. Should we ❸ _____ , too?

Sasha: Why not? The more the merrier.

Robert: I can't believe it. People are even dancing on the tables. Is that really a local ❹ _____ ?

Sasha: Sure. People do it ❺ _____ during Oktoberfest. Just don't fall!

Robert: I always thought German people were so serious all the time.

Sasha: As you can see, that's just a ❻ _____ . Once you get to know the German people, they're really warm and welcoming.

Robert: I can see that. This is such a ❼ _____ ❽ _____ . I want to sing along with the next song the band plays!

Sasha: Hold on, I'd better teach you the words first.

Words to Remember

Choose the words in the box to complete the following sentences.

join in	festive	custom	stereotype
gathering	blend in	all the time	stick out

1. With his long hair, Jake _____ among his short-haired friends.
2. To _____ with the locals, Ted learned their language.
3. French people aren't rude. That's just a _____ .
4. Showing good hospitality is a _____ of my people.
5. We'll be having a small _____ at our place—just a few people.

Get It Right

We use prepositions of time when we talk about what we are going to do, or what we have already done.

Example:

I arrived at the festival at four p.m. My friend got there on Friday night.

Your Turn: Pretend you're are writing a letter to a friend about your experience attending a festival in a foreign country. Use prepositions of time to describe what you did and when you did it.

_____

_____

_____

Grammar Bite

Prepositions of time are used before days, months, years, and any other words that have to do with the passage of time. Prepositions of time include *at*, *in*, and *on*. *At* is used before specific times, such as "three o'clock," or general times, such as "day" or "night." *In* goes before "morning," "afternoon," and "evening," as well as before months, seasons, or years. *On* goes before dates, days of the week, or single-day events.

Examples:

- We're leaving *at* five o'clock.
- The Tomatina is held *in* August.
- We got here *on* Tuesday.
- My flight leaves *at* night.

Give It a Try

Complete the following sentences with the prepositions of time in the box.

in	*on*	*at*

1. My boss from New York will arrive   ON   Monday.
2. The train will get here _____ 3:30 p.m.
3. My wife and I were married _____ September.
4. These animals only come out _____ night.
5. The company was founded _____ 2009.

🎈 Prepare Yourself

Look at the pictures of various festivals around the world.

Las Fallas in Spain

Songkran in Thailand

Tomatina in Spain

St. Patrick's Day in Ireland

Running of the Bulls in Spain

Oktoberfest in Germany

🎈 Activity 1

With a partner, take turns answering the following questions about the pictures above.

1. Do you like to "Do as the Romans do" when you travel? Why or why not?
2. What is the hardest part of blending in with the locals when traveling?
3. What is your favorite kind of festival and why?
4. What is the best way to learn local customs at a festival?

🎈 Activity 2

Look at the pictures again. Try searching on the Internet for more information about each festival. Take notes on the things you would like to do at the festival, as well as how you would blend in and get to know the local people. Then explain what you would do to a partner.

🎈 Useful Expressions

- In order to blend in, I'd try *speaking a bit of German with some of the locals*.
- Local people really appreciate it when you make an effort to get to know their *culture*.
- *Music* is a universal language, so singing and dancing or just talking about music could be a good start.
- Making a bit of *small talk* is a good way to start a cultural exchange.

Unit 15

Buying Souvenirs

By the end of this unit, you will be able to do the following:

→ Talk about buying souvenirs
→ Ask a souvenir shop clerk questions about souvenirs
→ Bargain in a flea market
→ Use your linguistic skills to get the best possible price

Before We Go

Look at the following pictures of things you would commonly find in a souvenir shop. Match the pictures (1-6) with the proper terms in the box.

| stuffed animal | towel | figurine | hat | postcard | T-shirt |

❶ _____

❷ _____

❸ _____

❹ _____

❺ _____

❻ _____

Useful Expressions

- How much is this *mug*?
- Could you give me *a better price*?

- Is there a *discount* if I buy more than one?
- Does this *cap* come in another color / size?

Conversation 1

Track 48 Wayne and his friend Erin are looking to buy some souvenirs. They've come to a large flea market, and are wandering amongst the various stalls and shops. Listen to the conversation and fill in the missing words.

Wayne: What kind of souvenir do you want to get?

Erin: I want to get something ❶ _____ . Everyone always comes home with a T-shirt or a mug. I want something ❷ _____ .

Wayne: There's a shop over there selling commemorative plates. That's kind of different.

Erin: I'd probably have to ❸ _____ something that ❹ _____ home, and there's no way I'm paying for that.

Wayne: OK, let's see. Something you can pack in your backpack. Hey, over there. That guy is selling mini replica statues of Michelangelo's *David*.

Erin: Now you're talking. Whenever I look at it, I'll be reminded of seeing the real thing.

Wayne: I wonder if we can ❺ _____ with the guy.

Erin: This is a flea market. I'm pretty sure we can. But I think he'll ❻ _____ .

Wayne: Then we'll just have to be tough. Have you ever haggled before?

Erin: Once or twice. He'll tell you the price, then you make an ❼ _____ . He'll make a ❽ _____ , and eventually you'll make a deal.

Wayne: That doesn't sound too hard. Shall we give it a try?

Erin: Sure, I'll follow your lead.

Words to Remember

Choose the words in the box to complete the sentences.

ship	haggle	different	special
fragile	offer	counter-offer	drive a hard bargain

1. If you want to get a good price, you'll have to _____ .

2. The shop owner _____ , but he is fair.

3. If you really want to buy this, I can give you a good price. Make me an _____ .

4. Be careful with that souvenir statue. It's made of glass, so it is _____ .

5. I don't want to buy the same souvenir as you. I want something _____ .

Reading

⚫Track 49 Read this article about the proper way to haggle.

Haggling is a bit of a lost art these days. One recent study shows that, in the past three years, less than 50 percent of people have tried to get a better price on something. But that doesn't mean haggling is dead—far from it. It's very much alive, and there are a few tips you should keep in mind the next time you try to make a deal.

If you're new to haggling, it doesn't hurt to have a script in your head before you try and make the deal. Map out how the conversation might go, and practice a bit before you actually go into the store. That way, you'll know just how to respond, and will sound confident. Secondly, do your research beforehand. Know exactly what you want to buy, and what the normal price for that item is. Without this information, you're basically at the seller's mercy. When the time does come to make an offer, don't offer a price that the seller would consider insulting. Go low, but not too low. Insult the seller, and negotiations could break down before they have a chance to begin. Don't be desperate to buy, and be prepared to walk away if you're not getting the price you want. That puts the power in your hands. You'd be surprised how often a better offer comes your way as you're taking your first steps out of the shop. Now get out there, and start haggling!

Give It a Try

A. Based on the article, circle True or False for the following sentences.

1. When shopping, appear desperate.   True / False
2. Never walk away from a deal.   True / False
3. Have a script of the deal in your head.   True / False
4. Insult the seller to gain respect.   True / False
5. Do research before you shop.   True / False

B. Based on the article, choose the correct answer for the following questions.

1. What does the article say about haggling?
   a. Not many people do it these days.
   b. It is a lost art.
   c. It has been illegal for three years.
   d. No one does it anymore.

2. What will having a script in your head help you do?
   a. Stay awake   **c.** Remain stressed
   b. Be confident   **d.** Sound interested

3. What could happen if you make an offer that is too low?
   a. It could get you a really low price.   **c.** It could start the negotiation off well.
   b. It could make the seller laugh.   **d.** It could anger the seller.

Conversation 2

Track 50 Wayne and Erin are now inside the shop selling the mini replica statues. The clerk comes to greet them. Listen to the conversation and fill in the missing words.

Clerk: Hi there, can I help you?

Wayne: Hello, we're just looking, thanks.

Erin: What are you talking about, we came in here specifically to get a…

Wayne: Keep it down, we don't want to look too
❶ _____. That gives her the
❷ _____ in the ❸ _____.

Erin: Oh, I get it. Uh, yeah, we're just having a look around.

Wayne: Those replicas of Michelangelo's David look all right.
❹ _____?

Clerk: Well, normally go for $30, but I'm open to offers.

Erin: Hmm, $30. That's ❺ _____. Not bad at all. But what would you say to $15?

Clerk: I'd say that's ❻ _____. I'd be
❼ _____ it _____ at that price.

Wayne: Then I think $20 is a good ❽ _____. Wouldn't you agree?

Clerk: Hmm, yeah, why not. $20 it is.

Erin: Awesome, here you go.

Words to Remember

Choose the words in the box to complete the following sentences.

| too low / high | negotiation | compromise | not bad |
| advantage | eager | how much | give away |

1. After finishing school, Harold is _____ to start his career.
2. Mary has the _____ when playing basketball because she is very tall.
3. That shirt looks nice. _____?
4. I won't pay $30 for that CD. That's _____.
5. The singer and the record company are in the middle of a contract _____.

Get It Right

We often use intensifiers when we are negotiating.

Example:

That price is too high. Can't you do better?

Your Turn: Pretend you are negotiating via e-mail with a seller for something you want to buy. Use as many intensifiers as you can to make your case for the lowest possible price. You can use intensifiers to describe the seller's first offer, to describe the product you want to buy, and anything else you can think of.

_____

_____

_____

_____

Grammar Bite

We use intensifiers to make adjectives stronger, or to modify nouns or even adverbs. Here are some basic intensifiers that are commonly used.

Too is used to show that there is a lot of something. You can use *too* before an adjective.

Example:

• It is *too* cold outside.

Enough means that you have what you need, and goes before a noun.

Example:

• There are *enough* sandwiches for everyone at the party.

So means very, and is generally placed before an adverb or an adjective.

Example:

• It's *so* hot that I just want to stay indoors.

Such also means very. It is used before an adjective and a noun.

Example:

• It's *such* a nice day outside.

Give It a Try

Complete the following sentences with the prepositions of time in the box.

| too   enough   so   such |

1. Tony thinks he's had ~~enough~~ drinks.
2. It's _____ windy there are trees falling down.
3. It's _____ dark to see in here.
4. Chris is _____ a nice guy that he always helps his friends.
5. The sun is _____ bright. It hurts my eyes.

Prepare Yourself

Look at the pictures below of shoppers looking around at a flea market.

Activity 1

With a partner, take turns answering the following questions about the pictures above.

1. What kinds of souvenirs do you prefer to buy and why?
2. Do you factor souvenirs into your travel budget? Why or why not?
3. Do you enjoy haggling over a price? Why or why not?
4. Do you consider yourself a good haggler? Why or why not?

Activity 2

The above pictures were taken on Portobello Road in London, England, considered one of the world's greatest flea markets. Take a look at the various shops in the pictures, and take notes on which ones you would like to visit, as well as what you might like to buy there. Then, describe where you would go and what you would buy to a partner. Also, describe your haggling technique, or how you would get the best price possible.

Useful Expressions

- I would really like to pick up a *bobble-head doll*.
- I find *being friendly* with the vendor is a *good way to get the best price*.
- Some *street art* caught my eye.
- A *traditional costume* could be just the thing to commemorate my trip.

REVIEW 5

Listening

Track 51 You are going to hear a man and a woman talking in five different situations. Read the questions and then choose the correct answer, a, b, or c.

1. What does the woman offer to do?
   a. Sell the man a ticket at a discount.
   b. Pay for the man's museum ticket.
   c. Take the man around the museum.

2. What does the man say about dinosaurs?
   a. He's never been interested in them.
   b. He's been interested in them for a long time.
   c. He's very scared of them.

3. What does the man wonder about the Stone Age?
   a. Who was alive during the Stone Age.
   b. When the Stone Age happened.
   c. What life was like then.

4. What does the woman say about the vase?
   a. There are few real ones left.
   b. There aren't any fake ones left.
   c. There aren't any real ones left.

5. What will the man likely do next?
   a. Continue his tour
   b. Buy a souvenir
   c. Complain about the museum

Vocabulary

Choose the correct words to complete the sentences.

impress	local	architect	design

1. This bowl is thousands of years old, but it's still in perfect *(condition / collection)*.

2. Take a look at this artifact. It was dug up at a *(age / site)* not far from here.

3. Check out this interesting book. It's about how people lived in *(ancient / preserved)* times.

4. The people working at the museum aren't paid. They're *(exhibitions / volunteers)*.

5. I'd like two *(tickets / donations)*, please.

Grammar

Complete the following sentences with the correct prepositions of time.

1. We will leave _____ four o'clock.

2. I have a doctor's appointment _____ Monday.

3. The concert will be _____ June.

4. Will your birthday party be during the day or _____ night?

5. The last time I took a vacation was _____ 2010.

Reading

Complete the words in the text. The first letters are given.

What's the best and most fun way to meet local people when you're traveling? Try attending a fest_____. These are occasions when people get together, listen to music, eat great food, and just generally have a good time. It's a great way to get to know the cult_____ of a place. When I was traveling through the Boston, I went to a festival that celebrated the city's rich history. There were people everywhere dressed in trad_____ clothing. It was really interesting to see how people dressed in the pa_____. And on one stage, a band played some old fo_____ music. Some people in the crowd taught me the words, and I was even invited on stage to sing. What an experience!

Writing

Pretend you want to buy something online. The problem is, you think the price is too high. Write an email (150-190 words) telling the seller that you want to negotiate, and do your best to convince the seller to lower the price. You can use intensifiers (Unit 15) to strengthen your case. Look at the e-mail below as an example.

Dear sir,

I'm writing in regard to the flat-screen television you have advertised for sale on www.sellstuff.com. I like what I see. The size is just right for my apartment, and I like the fact that it's only a couple of years old. However, I think you might be asking too high a price. $500 just isn't reasonable for a two-year-old television. I've done some price comparisons, and it seems like $300 is a fairer price. I think that's something we can both live with. If you insist on leaving the price where it is, I'll probably have to walk away from this one. But this is a negotiation, so feel free to throw another number at me. I'm sure we'll be able to work something out. Hopefully, we can do business together. Thanks for your time, and I look forward to hearing from you.

Sincerely,
Brad Johnson

Unit 1 My Travel Plans

Look at the following activities that people enjoy doing on vacation. Match each word from the box with the activity.

| hiking | sailing | sightseeing | skiing | swimming | visiting museums |

❶

❷

❸

❹

❺

❻

Useful Expressions

- I'd like to take a vacation *in the city* because I like to *visit the museums*.
- *The beach* looks best to me because I *like surfing*.
- I enjoy *hiking*, so I think I would like a vacation *in the mountains* the best.
- I will arrive in *Rome* on *July 26*. At *10:00* on the first day, I will *go to the Vatican Museum*.
- Next, I will go to *the Pantheon*. There, I can *have lunch*.
- I really want to visit *Spanish Steps* because I love *watching people*.

Unit 2 What Should I Bring?

Look at the following activities that people enjoy doing on vacation. Match each word from the box with the activity.

| suitcase | backpack | clothing | toothbrush | sunglasses | passport |

① _____

② _____

③ _____

④ _____

⑤ _____

⑥ _____

🎈 Useful Expressions

- What is in your *suitcase*?
- I have a *hairdryer* in my *suitcase*.
- What is that next to the *toothbrush*?
- I think you should also bring your *sunglasses*.

- I could not live without *a hairdryer*.
- *A water bottle* would be useful on any trip.
- I would bring *socks* and *a toiletry bag*.
- I would also bring along *some books*.

Unit 3 Catching a Plane

Look at the pictures in an airport terminal below. There are several places marked with the numbers 1-6. Match these places to the correct words from the box.

check-in desk   moving sidewalk   security screening
customs and immigration baggage claim   duty free

①

②

③

④ _____ ⑤ _____ ⑥ _____

🎈 Useful Expressions

- Before you go to the *airport* you need to have *all your travel documents*.
- When you go to *check-in*, make sure you have your *passport* ready.
- After you *check-in*, go to the *security screening checkpoint*.
- While *you're waiting at the gate, read a book* or *listen to music* to pass the time.

Unit 4

Checking In / Out

Look at the pictures below of a hotel. Match the numbered pictures (1-6) with the correct term

| *receptionist* | *reception desk* | *bellhop* | *luggage cart* | *elevator* | *key card* |

❶ _____

❷ _____

❸ _____

❹ _____

❺ _____

❻ _____

- Do you have a *reservation*?
- Could I see your *ID*, please?
- Can I have a wake-up call *tomorrow*?
- Do you have any *rooms* available?

- I'd like to *check in*.
- How long will you be *staying with us*?
- How would you like to *pay*?
- I'd like a *single / double room / shared dorm*.

🎈 Unit 5 Meeting Roommates

Look at the pictures of a hostel dorm room below. Match the numbered items (1-6) with the correct term in the box.

| **bunk bed** | **closet** | **bathroom** | **nightstand** | **roommate** |

①   ②   ③

④   ⑤

🎈 Useful Expressions

- Hello, nice to meet you, my name is *Josh*.
- Where *are you* from?
- How long have you been *traveling*?
- What do you do *back home*?

- It's great to meet *you*.
- How *are you* doing?
- What *are your* favorite things to do?
- Tell me about *your family*.

Housekeeping

Unit 6

Look at the pictures of various cleaning supplies below. Match the numbered items (1-6) with the correct term in the box.

| *scrub* | *brush* | *glass cleaner fluid* | *rag* | *dustpan* | *broom* |

① _____

② _____

③ _____

④ _____

⑤ _____

⑥ _____

Useful Expressions

- Can you pass me the *mop*, please?
- I'll get started on the *bathroom*. You can *make the beds*.
- Be sure to *give the floor a good scrubbing*.
- Spray some cleaning solution on the *table* and wipe it off.

- You can start by *taking out the trash*.
- Then, move on to the *living room*.
- Don't forget to *vacuum the carpet*.
- Once you've *mopped the floor*, you'll have to dry it.

Buying Groceries

Unit 7

Look at the pictures of these common items we might buy at a grocery store. Match the numbered items (1-6) with the correct term in the box.

| *cereal* | *vegetables* | *meat* | *milk* | *bread* | *fruit* |

❶ _____   ❷ _____   ❸ _____

❹ _____   ❺ _____   ❻ _____

 Unit 8

Eating at a Market

Look at the pictures of these common foods and drinks we might find at a traditional market, or farmers market. Match the numbered items (1-10) with the correct term in the box.

potatoes	onions	meringue	apples	cheese
olives	spices	sweets	cherries	nuts

❶   ❷   ❸   ❹   ❺

113

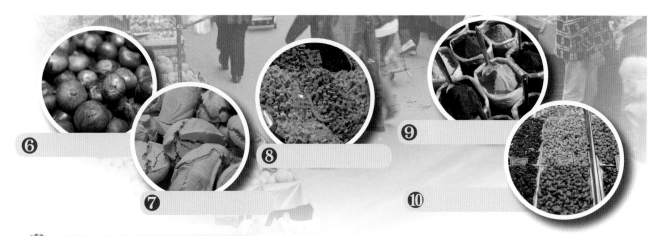

⑥　⑦　⑧　⑨　⑩

🎈 Useful Expressions

- I'm going to get *a bag of chestnuts* from this *stall / vendor*.
- I'm in the mood for something *salty*.
- Let's see what the other *vendors* have to offer.
- I'm going to see if I can *haggle for a better price*.
- First, I would visit the *vegetable stand* to get some *cucumbers*.
- I like *spicy dishes*, so I'd have to pick up some *peppers*.
- Next, I'd head for the *fruit stand* for some *apples*. They're a little bit *sweet*.
- Finally, I'd go to the *bakery* for some *fresh bread*. It's soft and *delicious*.

Unit 9 Eating at a Coffee Shop

Look at the pictures of these common foods are drinks we might order at a coffee shop. Match the numbered items (1-6) with the correct term in the box.

donut　sandwich　muffin　croissant　coffee　tea

❶　❷　❸

❹　❺　❻

Useful Expressions

- What would you like today?
- I'll have *a ham and cheese sandwich and a large black coffee*, please.
- Would you like anything else?
- Your total comes to *$4.75*.
- I want to get something *sweet / healthy*.
- I like *black coffee* because it is *bitter*.
- The *bagels* here are especially good.
- This shop's specialty is the *café mocha*, so I'll have to order one of those.

Unit 10 — Getting Around the City

Look at the pictures of these common kinds of transportation that we encounter in a trip. Match the numbered items (1-6) with the correct term in the box.

airplane   bus   ferry   subway   taxi   train

❶   ❷   ❸

❹   ❺   ❻

Useful Expressions

- What do you see on the front of the *bus*?
- I can see the route number. It's *number 10*.
- What does the *bus stop* sign say?
- The *bus* is heading toward the Potsdam Square.
- I will begin my tour at *Park Güell*.

- From there, I will take *the bus* to *Casa Mila*.
- I will get out at *Girona* station and *walk to the next sight*.
- I will end my day at *Sagrada Família*.

Unit 11 Where Am I?

Look at the following pictures of direction signs. Match the pictures (1-5) with the correct term in the box.

| stop | turn around / turn back | go straight | turn right | turn left |

❶ _____   ❷ _____   ❸ _____   ❹ _____   ❺ _____

 Useful Expressions

- Excuse me, can you tell me how to get to the *Natural History museum*?
- Go straight for *two blocks* and then *turn right*.
- I was wondering if you could tell me how to get to the *library*.
- Pardon me, I seem to be lost.
- I would start my day at the *Eiffel tower*.
- From there, I would walk *two blocks east* to the *Louvre Museum*.
- After that, I would head *south* toward *the Arc de Triomphe*.
- Finally, I would walk *three blocks left, turn right*, and end my day at *the Grand Palais*.

Unit 12 I'm Sick

Look at these pictures of a few symptoms of common illnesses. Match the pictures (1-6) to the proper terms in the box.

| stomachache | earache | headache | sore throat | runny nose | coughing / sneezing |

❶ _____   ❷ _____   ❸ _____

④ ⑤ ⑥

 Useful Expressions

- I haven't been feeling well the past couple of *days*.
- My *throat* is *sore*.
- I'm *coughing* all the time.
- I have a *pounding headache*.
- First, I would check in at the reception desk.
- Next, I would have a seat in the waiting room.
- Eventually, a nurse would call my number.
- After seeing the doctor, I would pick up my prescription.

Unit 13 Museums for Free

Look at the following pictures of things you would commonly find in a museum. Match the pictures (1-6) with the proper terms in the box.

| artifacts | guide | sculpture | ticket booth | display | souvenirs |

① ② ③

④ ⑤ ⑥

💬 Useful Expressions

- This *display* comes from the *Cambrian period*.
- What are these interesting *artifacts*?
- Do you know how old this *statue* is?
- When was this *settlement* discovered?
- The *Vikings exhibition* is a must-see, as *the Vikings are part of my family heritage*.
- I've always been interested in *money*, so I have to wander through *the ancient coins exhibit*.
- *Egypt* has fascinated me for a long time, so I have to check out the artifacts taken from *King Tut's tomb*.
- The exhibition on *medieval Japan* should be interesting. I'm intrigued by *Japanese culture*.

Unit 14 Do As the Romans Do

Look at the following pictures of things you would commonly find at a local cultural festival. Match the pictures (1-6) with the proper terms in the box.

food stand	stage	costume	parade	flag	band

❶

❷

❸

❹

❺

❻

Useful Expressions

- What time will the *performance* begin?
- What is the cultural significance of this *display*?
- How did *the festival* get started?
- Can you help me understand *what's going on here*?
- In order to blend in, I'd try *speaking a bit of German with some of the locals.*
- Local people really appreciate it when you make an effort to get to know their *culture.*
- *Music* is a universal language, so singing and dancing or just talking about music could be a good start.
- Making a bit of *small talk* is a good way to start a cultural exchange.

Unit 15 Buying Souvenirs

Look at the following pictures of things you would commonly find in a souvenir shop. Match the pictures (1-6) with the proper terms in the box.

stuffed animal　　*towel*　　*figurine*　　*hat*　　*postcard*　　*T-shirt*

❶ ____________

❷ ____________

❸ ____________

❹ ____________

❺ ____________

❻ ____________

Useful Expressions

- How much is this *mug*?
- Could you give me *a better price*?
- Is there *a discount* if I buy more than one?
- Does this *cap* come in another color / size?
- I would really like to pick up a *bobble-head doll.*
- I find *being friendly* with the vendor is a *good way to get the best price.*
- Some *street art* caught my eye.
- A *traditional costume* could be just the thing to commemorate my trip.

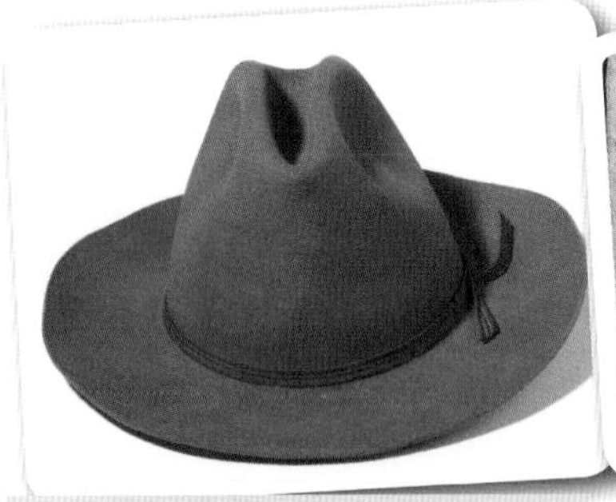

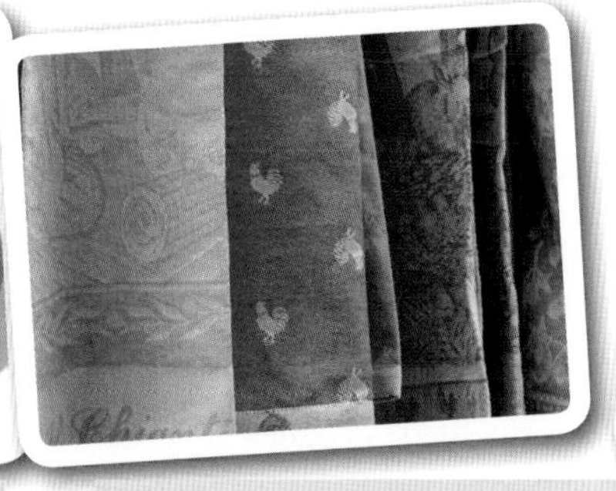

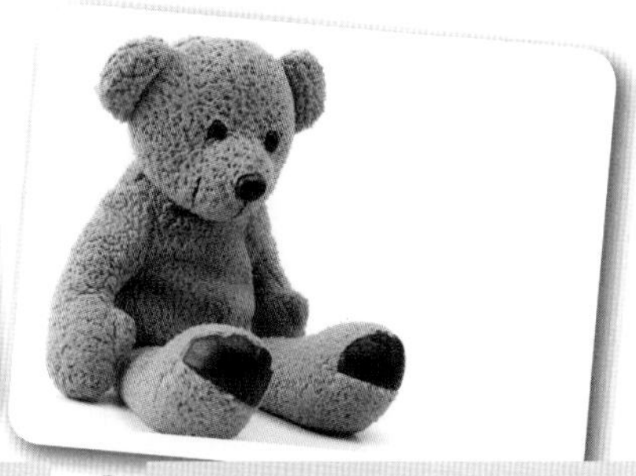

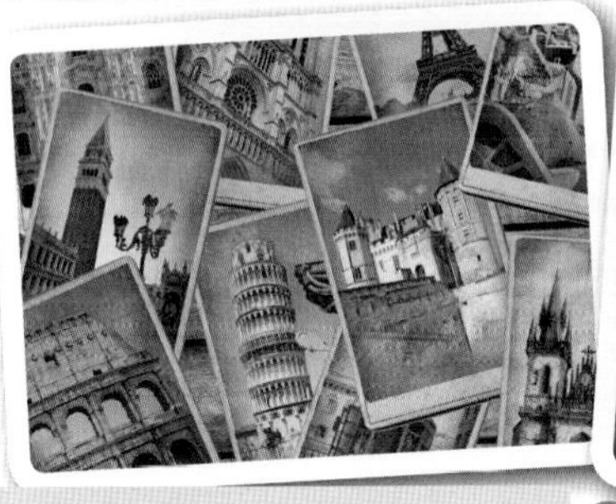

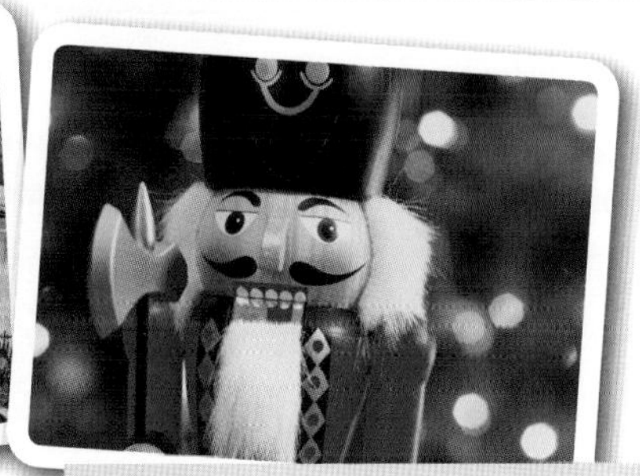

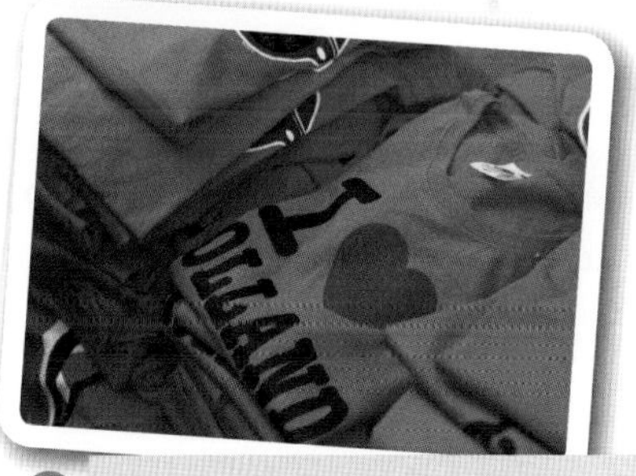

Photo credits

Cover Photos: iStockphoto/Thinkstock

Page 8: (l, 3-6) iStockphoto/Thinkstock, (2) Fuse/Thinkstock; **9:** iStockphoto/Thinkstock; **10:** Fuse/Thinkstock; **11-13:** iStockphoto/Thinkstock; **14:** (1-3, 5) iStockphoto/Thinkstock, (4) Ingram Publishing/Thinkstock, (6) Creatas/Thinkstock; **15:** Digital Vision/Thinkstock; **16:** iStockphoto/Thinkstock; **17:** (t) iStockphoto/Thinkstock, (m) Hemera/Thinkstock, (b) Purestock/Thinkstock; **18:** Ingram Publishing/Thinkstock; **19:** (knife) Purestock/Thinkstock, (noodles) Stockbyte/Thinkstock, (others) iStockphoto/Thinkstock; **20:** (1) iStockphoto/Thinkstock, (2, 4-6) Digital Vision/Thinkstock, (3) TongRo Images/Thinkstock; **21:** iStockphoto/Thinkstock; **22:** Creatas/Thinkstock; **23:** (t) Creatas/Thinkstock, (m) iStockphoto/Thinkstock, (b) Image Source/Thinkstock; **24:** iStockphoto/Thinkstock; **25:** (lost) BananaStock/Thinkstock, (working) Valueline/Thinkstock, (security, shopping) iStockphoto/Thinkstock, (others) Digital Vision/Thinkstock; **26:** iStockphoto/Thinkstock; **28:** iStockphoto/Thinkstock; **29:** (t) Fuse/Thinkstock, (b) Digital Vision/Thinkstock; **30:** iStockphoto/Thinkstock; **31:** Photodisc/Thinkstock; **32:** iStockphoto/Thinkstock; **33:** (info) Stockbyte/Thinkstock, (lockers) Zoonar/Thinkstock, (others) iStockphoto/Thinkstock; **34:** (1) Ingram Publishing/Thinkstock, (2, 4-5) iStockphoto/Thinkstock, (3) Fuse/Thinkstock ; **35:** (t) Wavebreak Media/Thinkstock, (b) iStockphoto/Thinkstock; **36:** Stockbyte/Thinkstock; **37:** iStockphoto/Thinkstock; **39:** (center) iStockphoto/Thinkstock, (pizza) Image Source/Thinkstock, (chatting, relaxing, discussing) Digital Vision/Thinkstock, (nap, music) Photodisc/Thinkstock; **40:** (1-3, 5-6) iStockphoto/Thinkstock, (4) Hemera/Thinkstock; **41-42:** Digital Vision/Thinkstock; **43-44:** iStockphoto/Thinkstock; **45:** (laundry, floor) Ingram Publishing/Thinkstock, (sink) iStockphoto/Thinkstock, (window) Wavebreak Media/Thinkstock, (dishes) moodboard/Thinkstock, (vacuum) Digital Vision/Thinkstock; **46:** iStockphoto/Thinkstock; **48:** (1, 6) iStockphoto/Thinkstock, (2) Digital Vision/Thinkstock, (3-4) Purestock/Thinkstock; **49:** (t) iStockphoto/Thinkstock, (b) Digital Vision/Thinkstock; **50:** iStockphoto/Thinkstock; **51:** (t) iStockphoto/Thinkstock, (b) Purestock/Thinkstock; **52:** Wavebreak Media/Thinkstock; **53:** (milk, jam) Tetra images/Thinkstock, (others) iStockphoto/Thinkstock; **54:** (1, 4-5, 7, 10) iStockphoto/Thinkstock, (2, 9) Digital Vision/Thinkstock, (3) Purestock/Thinkstock, (6) moodboard/Thinkstock, (8) Ingram Publishing/Thinkstock; **55:** (t) iStockphoto/Thinkstock, (b) Ingram Publishing/Thinkstock; **56-59:** iStockphoto/Thinkstock; **60:** iStockphoto/Thinkstock; **61:** (t) Fuse/Thinkstock, (m, b) iStockphoto/Thinkstock ; **62-64:** iStockphoto/Thinkstock; **65:** (writing) Blend Images/Thinkstock, (studying) Stockbyte/Thinkstock, (others) iStockphoto/Thinkstock; **66:** iStockphoto/Thinkstock; **68:** (1, 3-6) iStockphoto/Thinkstock, (2) Stockbyte/Thinkstock; **69-72, 74:** iStockphoto/Thinkstock; **75:** (t) Digital Vision/Thinkstock, (b) iStockphoto/Thinkstock; **76:** Digital Vision/Thinkstock; **77-78:** iStockphoto/Thinkstock; **79:** (t) Purestock/Thinkstock, (b) iStockphoto/Thinkstock; **80:** (1-5) iStockphoto/Thinkstock, (6) Wavebreak Media/Thinkstock; **81:** iStockphoto/Thinkstock; **82:** Digital Vision/Thinkstock; **83-84:** iStockphoto/Thinkstock; **85:** (back pain) Creatas/Thinkstock, (neck pain) moodboard/Thinkstock, (arm) Fuse/Thinkstock, (ankle) iStockphoto/Thinkstock, (allergy) Wavebreak Media/Thinkstock; **86:** iStockphoto/Thinkstock; **88:** (1, 5-6) iStockphoto/Thinkstock, (2, 4) Photodisc/Thinkstock, (3) Fuse/Thinkstock; **89:** (t) iStockphoto/Thinkstock, (b) Photodisc/Thinkstock; **90:** iStockphoto/Thinkstock; **91:** (t) iStockphoto/Thinkstock, (m) Stockbyte/Thinkstock; **92:** iStockphoto/Thinkstock; **93:** (center) Fuse/Thinkstock, (sculptures) TongRo Images/Thinkstock, (plants, animal, industry) iStockphoto/Thinkstock, (painting) Stockbyte/Thinkstock, (literature) Hemera/Thinkstock; **94-95:** iStockphoto/Thinkstock; **96:** Stockbyte/Thinkstock; **97:** (t) iStockphoto/Thinkstock, (m) iStock Editorial/Thinkstock; **98:** (t) iStockphoto/Thinkstock, (m) Getty Images News/Thinkstock; **99:** (Las Fallas,) iStockphoto/Thinkstock, (Songkran, Tomatina, St. Patrick's Day, Running of the Bulls) Getty Images News/Thinkstock, (Oktoberfest) AbleStock.com/Thinkstock; **100:** (1) Purestock/Thinkstock, (2) Hemera/Thinkstock, (3-4, 6) iStockphoto/Thinkstock, (5) Purestock/Thinkstock; **101:** iStockphoto/Thinkstock; **102:** Digital Vision/Thinkstock; **103:** (t) iStockphoto/Thinkstock, (m) iStock Editorial/Thinkstock, (b) BananaStock/Thinkstock; **104:** Fuse/Thinkstock; **105:** (jewelry, pots, furniture, bags, used clothes, dishware) iStockphoto/Thinkstock, (coins, watches) Zoonar/Thinkstock; **106:** iStockphoto/Thinkstock.